My Spiritual

Journey of

H~old~ O~n~ P~ain~ E~nds~

Deborah Eaddy-Warren

Cover and interior design by Sable Books

ISBN 978-0-9987810-3-7

Sable Books
sablebooks.org

Contents

I dedicate this book to several People. First to my mother Nina Eaddy who challenged me to make a life for myself. Second to my husband Joseph Warren, Jr. for always encouraging and helping me succeed at whatever I put my mind to do, and to my daughter Latisha Eaddy, thank you for accepting and carrying out the bar I set so high for you. Lastly, to Jaki Shelton-Green for pushing me to keep writing this book every time I wanted to give up.

Preface

Sixteen and pregnant! What was I going to do?

When I finally got the nerve to tell my mom she was upset. She said she already knew because of the way I looked. Then she hit me with words so hard I felt like she had hit me upside my head with a bat.

"You will never be good for nothing. You will just have baby after baby."

As I sat there with my head pounding, the words rang loud in my head. I said to myself, I'll show her.

Then one day she came to me and said she had spoken with the pastor and his wife and they wanted to adopt the baby. I couldn't breathe. I just sat there trying to breathe.

"Think about it and let me know what you decide," she said. "But if you decide to keep the baby, it will be your responsibility to take care of it."

I could breathe again. She had challenged me when she said I would never be good for nothing, and I was determined to prove her wrong.

I wrote this book in part because I want to inspire young mothers to follow their dreams. I also want to inspire all people struggling with life. If I accomplished all I did after becoming a "statistic" and with my mother saying that I would never be good for nothing, you can too.

The good thing is that it's never too late to accomplish your dream. If only one person's life is changed by my story, I have accomplished my goal. I pray that my story will change many lives. Don't let making a mistake at an early age keep you from accomplishing your goals and dreams. Don't be a victim for life. Trust God and be a victor.

I am a victor now, but I was a victim for over thirty years. Anger controlled me and I was an emotional wreck. The pain, the hurt, and the shame overwhelmed me, and I made bad decisions. I allowed my negative emotions to keep me in fear. When I started trusting God, my negative emotions little by little died, and His blessings started flowing.

God guided me through the storms of my bad decisions, turning me toward successful results. I am who I am today because I started trusting God's voice and eventually dismissed the negative thoughts and words my mom said that stuck in my head for so many years.

Chapter 1

From a Child's View

Everyone was at grandma's house. I had on my Sunday best dress, and while I can't recall the exact outfit, I know I had on shoes because the only time we wore shoes were when we were going somewhere. Grandma told me to sit still and not get dirty. I listened because I knew if I got dirty I would not be able to go, and Lord knows I didn't want her to leave me, so I sat on the couch and waited. I heard someone say the cars were lined up at the road. My grandma took my hand and we walked out to the road and got into one of the cars. I didn't understand what was going on, but I was with grandma, all dressed up, feeling pretty so nothing else mattered. Grandma was my world, and I was happiest when I was with her, especially when I had her all to myself. My Grandma spent most of her time in the kitchen. After she fed us breakfast, she would send us outside. Sometimes I'd come back in and watch her prepare meals, and help her make frozen ice pops in a cup. She would let me line up the cups. Then I would watch her pour the Kool-Aid into the cups, and then line them up in the freezer. She sold them for five cents a cup. The neighborhood kids were eager to get them on a hot summer day. We brought some too, but she was grandma so we were always able to get freebies.

The car dropped us off at the door and we went inside, found our seats, and sat down. No sooner than we sat down, and I snuggled underneath my grandma I notice people crying.

Oh Lord, why is everyone crying? What's going on? I don't feel like crying because I'm happy. I'm with grandma. Oh wow! Who was that who just passed out? What is happening? What are they doing? Why is that man holding that woman? More people pass out and others running to put that white thing under their noses. The people who passed out are waking up now. Oh no! Now tears are flowing from grandma's eyes. Now I'm praying that she doesn't pass out too. OH, GOD HELP ME! I'm too afraid to be without her.

Then a man stood up front and started talking. He said a lot of nice things about my uncle as he laid sleeping in the box. As he talked about my uncle, the people started crying again. Why are they crying now? The man didn't say anything bad. He finished talking then we all marched up front to look at my uncle in the box. Why was he still sleeping? With all the noise, why hasn't he wakened up? After we all marched around the box, they closed it. What was he doing in that box anyway, and why would they close it? Are those men crazy? How can he breathe? Then we all got back into the cars and drove to a place outdoors. There were chairs lined up with a covering on top. In front of the chairs was a big hole in the ground. What is going on? What was the hole for?

After everyone was seated or standing around the chairs, they brought the closed box my uncle was sleeping in and slowly lowered it into the hole after the man that spoke at the other place said a few more words. I started wailing and sobbing like a crazy person. I couldn't help myself. What are they doing, why did they put Uncle Coolidge in that hole? Why, why, why? My grandmother tried to explain that he was dead, and that's where people go when they died. I couldn't control my tears. I was sobbing so bad the snot was running from my nose, and I was having trouble breathing. I was so afraid I was going to pass out and they would put that white thing to my nose, but I couldn't stop the tears. All the tears I had saved up since they told us Uncle Coolidge had died came pouring out. All of a sudden, it all became clear why everyone was crying. They knew Uncle Coolidge was going to be put in the hole. My tears just kept pouring out. I probably could have filled a water bucket with all my tears. At five I didn't understand what death was. It probably would have been a little easier if grandma would have explained the process to me so I would have known what to expect.

Anyway, this beautiful woman came out of nowhere. I don't recall seeing her at the other place, but she came over and tried to help my grandma calm me down. It was the lady we called Aunt Nina. She had beautiful long hair, pretty brown skin, and was dressed in a beautiful black and white fitted dress. She was so beautiful and walked with an air that said she knew she was beautiful. Her shoes were black high heels, with rhinestones on them, and she had on this long flowing white coat, which flung open when she walked. I couldn't stop staring at her because people in our town didn't dress with such style. She was so beautiful. She was able to calm me down only because I was so in awe of her beauty.

Later, back at grandma's house, Aunt Nina came by, and when my sister saw her she ran over and gave her a big hug. She was so excited to see her. I just assumed everyone loved her because she was so beautiful. Then I heard her tell my sister, "I will be back to get you and your sister soon." I didn't understand why Aunt Nina would come back to get us? After she left my grandmother tried to explain that Aunt Nina was my mother, and she was going to take us to live with her. After being with my grandma for five and a half years, my mom who I didn't know as mom was going to take us with her. I told my grandmother I didn't want to go. My grandmother tried to explain that my mom just left us until she could find housing for us. It didn't make sense to me. Then to make things worse, my grandma, the only mother I knew said that she was not my real grandmother, but she loves me as if I was her own, and for me not to forget it. I didn't understand what she was saying, but she said Aunt Nina was my real mother and when she came back I would have to go. The more I thought about leaving my grandmother, the worse it made me feel. How could she take me away from the only mother I knew? My grandmother kept trying to comfort me. I begged her to keep me, but mom came and took me away.

Going to Uncle Coolidge's funeral was one of my earliest memories. I still don't understand why a five-year-old would be taken to a funeral but I was there. I still remember it like it was yesterday, and often wonder if being scared as a child had something to do with attending that funeral. Uncle Coolidge was the youngest and my mother was the oldest of three children. Their mom died when my mom was five, her sister was four, and Uncle Coolidge was two years old. My mom said after her mother died, she had to look after her brother and sister, especially Uncle Coolidge because he was so young. She also said her dad took them to live with Great grandpa Julius until he remarried. Uncle Coolidge and my mom were very close, and she valued his opinion. My mom told us that the last time she saw her brother alive, he told her it was time to take her children before we get too old. Six months after he died, she came back to get us.

Another early memory was sleeping in my iron crib in my grandparent's bedroom. It was grey and made of iron and I remember a couple of times hurting myself getting in and out. My mom had left me with my grandparents when I was three months old. That's the reason my grandma was the only mother I knew. Although I called her grandma, she was my mom. I was the apple of my grandparent's eyes, and they loved me and I loved them just as much, and I was so happy. I lived with my grandparents from the age of three months until I started school. They protected me from the evils of the world. They had a couple acres of land and that was my world.

It was a beautiful world, and a loving and caring environment. The house was filled with lots of people and lots of love. Altogether, my grandparents had sixteen children and many of their children and their children's children all lived in the same house. Aunts, uncles, and cousins all grew up like brothers and sisters. I was closest to the children my age. There were four of us around the same age. We hung out and played together in my grandparents' back yard under the big oak tree. Its leaves were like fans always waiting to provide a breeze when we needed it. The saddest day of my life was leaving all that love. I thought leaving my grandparents was the worst thing that could happen to me. I was angry with everybody. I was angry with my grandparents for making me go. I was angry with Aunt Nina for taking me. When I later found out that Uncle Coolidge was the one who talked her into taking us, I was angry with him even though he was dead.

My happiness was gone and I was angry for a long, long time.

Chapter 2

The Trip to New York

My mother lived in Brooklyn, New York, a drastic change from little Myrtle Beach, South Carolina. It was August 1961, and still very hot when my mom came back to get us. I cried and cried just like I did at Uncle Coolidge's funeral. I was holding onto my grandma, sobbing because I didn't want to leave my grandparents, especially my grandma. My grandmother tried to comfort me and said everything would be alright. But I knew everything wouldn't be alright because I wouldn't be in my safe place protected by my grandparents. I was so angry with them and couldn't stop crying. I was naïve because I never thought my grandparents would let Aunt Nina take me.

My mother's sister, her nephew, and a cousin also came with us. Her sister came to take care of us while my mom worked. Her nephew and cousin came to find jobs and start a new life.

I was still crying when we got to the bus station. We waited outside for the bus. This was my first trip to town. The bus finally came and we all got on. It was a long bus ride to New York. We left early in the day, road all day and night and arrived early the next morning. I kept asking, "When are we going to get there?" My mom kept saying, "Soon".

I slept, woke up, and still we were not there. Finally, we arrived in Times Square. People were everywhere! I had never seen so many people in all my life. It was overwhelming and frightening. I wanted to turn around get back on the bus and go back to grandma. I felt like a little lost kid wandering around a crowd of strangers not knowing which way to go. Everyone looked so big. I was so small and frightened by all the big people moving fast past me. I was holding tight to my Aunt's hand as we walked through the bus station. I couldn't stop wondering where all the people came from. Then all of a sudden, we came to a huge, moving staircase. I had never seen anything like it. A lot of stairs, going straight up, and I could see no end. No way I was getting on. I started backing up, screaming.

"NO! NO! I'm scared!"

I refused to get on. Finally, my mother just dragged me on the moving stairs kicking and screaming. The stairs started moving and I almost fell backwards and she had to grab me. The stairs tried to eat my foot when I was getting off and I started screaming harder, crying out of control. Mom told me to shut up but I couldn't stop crying because I was so scared. This happened two or three more times, still crying, and angry at my mom because she kept dragging me on. We finally got rid of the moving stairs and then arrived at this noisy train station. Still, people everywhere. More people than I had seen in my five-and-a-half-year-old life time.

We stood on the platform waiting for the train to come. It finally came making a loud screeching noise before it came to a stop. I was so scared but after being dragged two or three times onto the moving stairs, I quietly got on the train for the ride to our new home. The train kept making stops and making that loud screeching noise as it came to each stop. It seemed like hours went by before we finally arrived. I remember the apartment very well. As you walked through the door there was a small hallway and bathroom across from it. The kitchen was to the left and a smaller bedroom was to the left of it. The living room was to the right of the door and a larger bedroom was across from it. This was my new room that I would share with my sister and aunt. It wasn't Grandma's but it was home, and wow, we had a bathroom.

By the end of the first day, I was homesick. I made the mistake of calling my mom Aunt Nina.

"Girl I am not your Aunt Nina. I'm your momma. Call me mom."

She was upset and I was angry at her because she yelled. I told her I wanted to go home. She said, "I am your momma and this is your home". But I was missing my grandmother and the comfort and security of my crib. I cried a lot. I begged my sister to write a letter asking our dad to send money for me to come home. When we lived with our grandparents, he would visit and give us money. I just assumed if we wrote, he would send the money. I was only there one day and I hated New York. I hated being away from my grandparents. I was a little country bumpkin.

The people in the apartment building thought my country accent was so cute. Every time I talked, they laughed. This made me angry but they thought it was so cute and funny. August of 1961 seemed like the worst month of my life, and things didn't get any better for a long time.

One day this little boy shows up. He walked in the door and the first thing he did was kick me on the shin bone. It really hurt. He was wearing those hard walking shoes that we wore in the 60's and 70's. He did it several times before I got tired and gave him a whack he wouldn't forget. Too my surprise, this was my two-year-old bratty brother. He lived with his father's mother and came to visit us on weekends. He was so bad we couldn't wait for Sunday evenings. We clapped when his dad picked him up. His dad would just look at us as if to say, *He's not that bad.* But he was.

My brother was out of control. My mom couldn't do much with him. However, he learned quickly if he kicked or hit me I was going to fight back, so he left me alone. I didn't know anything about the terrible two's back then, but my brother was definitely one. He would pour water on my sister's new hairdo, and poke holes in her skirts. My sister wouldn't fight him. She would get so angry she would cry. I guess she didn't want to hurt her little brother. He was always sneaking up behind her and doing something. We didn't like him and didn't look forward to his weekend visits.

Chapter 3

My First Days of School

I sat around sad most of the time. I was hurt and angry because my grandparents didn't fight to keep me. Now mom was talking about sending me to school. I didn't want to go. I wanted to go back to my grandparents.

September came and it was time for school. My mom tried to prepare me but it was more than I could handle. The first day my mom got up and fixed us a big breakfast. I recall eggs being part of the breakfast because after I drank a glass of cold water, I threw them up. I guess I was nervous about my new adventure. My aunt took us to school. We arrived and my aunt took me to class. I saw all the white kids in my class and I freaked out. I started crying uncontrollably just like I did when I saw them put my uncle in the hole, and I wouldn't go in. The teacher gave us chairs and we sat outside the classroom. The entire time my aunt was trying to convince me to go to class but I couldn't handle all those evil people. She sat in the hallway with me all day.

I don't recall ever going to town as a young child until my trip to New York. The adults went to town, and the children stayed home. If we got sick we didn't go to the doctor my grandmother would make up one of her concoctions to make us feel better. Since we didn't go to town as children, the only time I saw white people was when Mr. Waterway came to our house to collect payment for merchandise my grandparents brought. Mr. Waterway sold appliances. He was nice and very friendly. He would even stop and play with us sometimes. But he must have been one of the good ones because I recall someone saying white people were evil, and we could never look them in the eye. So I was afraid of them, but not Mr. Waterway. It was later when I found out why we couldn't look them in the eye. We were considered inferior to them, and if we looked them in the eye they would harm us.

I also remember playing baseball in the backyard one day and my sister struck out. My aunt who was close in age with us was so mad she started yelling at her. I sneaked up behind her to hit her in my sisters' defense. All of a sudden I felt the bat hit me up side my head. As I was sneaking up behind my aunt, she swung the bat and it had to be hard because I felt it go WAP! I started crying, and everyone started crowding around me yelling because blood was gushing out. At the time it happened, my grandmother was just returning from town. I heard someone ask if she was going to take me to the hospital.

She looked at my head, and said, "No go get me some spider webs from the loft," and asked for a few other items. Shortly, the bleeding was stopped and I was fixed up. I still have the scar on the left side corner of my head.

At the time, I didn't know there wasn't a black hospital nearby, only white ones, and we were not allowed in the white hospital. That's why my grandmother had to do what she did. That's probably also why many of the babies were born in the house and delivered by midwives.

When my mother got home from work and my aunt told her I wouldn't go to class and that she had to sit in the hallway with me all day mom was angry and threatened to put a tag on me with my name and destination and put me on the bus back to my grandparents. I was so happy and excited, and ready to go – until I heard her say I would be going alone. Then I was scared and angry at her for even thinking of sending me alone. Besides, she knew I was too young for that. I begged my sister to come with me but my mother repeated that if I didn't go to school she would send me alone. I was terrified to think of having to travel alone with all those evil people. I promised I would go to class. The next day I tried it again. Mom fixed breakfast again but I still couldn't eat. She said I needed to eat something but it made me sick to my stomach. I went to school again without eating. After several days of getting sick, my mom stopped trying to make me eat. Besides, they always gave us a morning snack at school.

My aunt walked us to school. I walked into class trying to be brave. A little white girl, who was just trying to be friendly, touched me. But what did I know? I started crying uncontrollably and ran into the hallway to my aunt. My aunt and I spent another day in the hallway. This went on for several weeks before my mother finally put her foot down. She made up the tag with my name and destination that she had been threatening and packed my suitcase. Out of panic of having to travel alone, I promised again to stay in class.

The next day, my aunt took me to school and I went to the class. She left because I had promised to stay, and they all thought I would. I don't think I was there more than a half hour when I started crying uncontrollably because I realized my aunt was not in the hallway. I cried so hard the teacher sent for the principal. He came and tried to calm me down but the only way he could calm me down was to agree to take me home. Now here I am walking down the street with this big grey-haired white man holding my hand, looking like grandpa bear and baby bear. He talked all the way trying to keep me calm.

"So where is your mom?" he asked. I pointed to the block past the block where we lived.

"She walks down that block every morning"

"She goes to work?"

"Yes."

"Then who is home?"

"My Aunt. She lives with us."

He kept asking questions, and I kept answering them until we arrived. It was amazing to me, holding the hand of a white man, but I wanted to get home. As we walked, I thought about Mr. Waterway and realized all white people can't be bad. As we walked home I remembered my mom's words to put me on the bus alone. I was so frightened and angry and didn't know what to do but I just couldn't handle staying in class with all those white kids.

He knocked on the door, but we got no answer.

I knew if my aunt wasn't there, my mother's nephew was there because he worked nights.

"Knock again," I told him. I did not want to go back to class with all those white kids.

Finally, we heard my cousin say "WHO IS IT?" in an angry tone. The principle said his name.

My cousin opened the door. The principal told him what happened. After the principal left, my cousin started yelling at me for not staying in school after I promised. Then he said, "Wait until I get dressed, I am going to take you back and you better stay. YOU HEAR ME?"

This was not the outcome I was expecting. I answered "yes," in a meek voice. I was so scared of him because he was angry and wouldn't stop yelling. I had never seen him like this before. I just wanted to get away from him. It was probably because we woke him up. He walked me back to school, still yelling. When we got there, I just wanted to get away from him.

"DO YOU NEED ME TO WALK YOU TO CLASS?"

I replied again in a mousey voice. "No."

"YOU BETTER STAY."

I nodded and ran off to class.

I didn't know how I was going to handle it but I walked in and took my seat. Even though I was scare of the white kids, I was more scared and angry at the way my cousin was yelling. I stayed in school the rest of the day and went to class every day afterwards.

Later, after I started staying in school, my mom told me the suitcase was empty, and she had no intention of sending me back.

Chapter 4

Going Home to See Grandma

I got to see my grandparents the next summer and every summer thereafter until I was too rebellious to go. This time I was prepared for the screeching loud noise of the train ride, the moving stairs, and the bus trip home. My aunt came with us. Mom fried chicken for us, wrapped it in wax paper, and put it in a shoe box with some bread. She also gave us money to buy drinks to have with our chicken and bread. I was so excited to be going to see my grandparents and was looking forward to sleeping in my crib again. To my surprise, they had thrown it out and I had to sleep in the room with my cousins.

"You threw it out?" I said.

They said they threw it out because I was too big for it and too old to sleep in the room with them. However, it took me some years to understand. Even though I was glad to be there, the pain was building up inside and my chest hurt badly.

At the end of the summer, my aunt, sister, and I took the bus back to New York. I didn't want to leave my grandparents and was hoping they saw my pain and sadness and would let me stay. I missed my grandparents so much. Grandma looked sad too as she gave me a big hug. We didn't have phones in the 60's so we wrote letters to each other. My grandmother taught me so much and I was molded in her values.

Not long after we got back, my mom somehow got a message from one of her sisters that grandma was sick and needed my aunt to come back to take care of her. My aunt packed her bags and left. Later, we found out that my grandmother wasn't sick, but my mother's sister wanted my aunt to help her take care of her kids.

When my mom found out, she was livid. She was so angry with the both of them. She said, they didn't have to scheme and should have been women enough to tell her. They didn't talk for a long time.

I remember mom saying, "They will need me before I need them."

My mom was right. It was years later when my two aunts were traveling to Myrtle Beach when their car broke down not too far from our house. They called my cousin who took me back to school. He called my mom because he didn't have a place for them to stay. He and my mom went to pick them up. They had to stay with us several days before their car was repaired. This was the first time they had seen each other since they pulled their scheme.

Mom was cordial, even though neither of them apologized or even mentioned what they had done.

When they left, mom said, "See, I told you they would need me before I needed them."

By this time my mother's nephew and cousin had gotten their own apartment. We had no one to stay with us because my mom didn't get home until 10pm. She would leave home after she got us off to school and we didn't see her again until 10pm. So we didn't have much time with her until the weekends. I do remember each night when she got home she would come to our room and lead us in our prayers.

One night my mom came in to pray with us and I started crying uncontrollably. She asked what was wrong. I told her I was playing a game with one of the kids outside and I lost.

She told me that if I said my prayers that night my arm would fall off. She thought my reaction was so funny and started laughing. I sat there still crying looking frighten and trying to figure out why she was laughing. Then she said it wasn't true and made me say my prayers. I wiped my tears, got control of myself and repeated after mom my prayers. The next morning I was throwing the covers off as quickly as I could to see if I still had my arm. Thank God it was still there.

Mom hired the neighbor's daughter to babysit and feed us. The babysitter and her sister would come over and stay with us until mom came home. The sister's boyfriend would come over some nights. He was a friend of the family so I guess my mom thought it was okay. However, when he got drunk he acted crazy. One night I was coming out of the bathroom. He grabbed me by the back of my skirt so hard, he grabbed my skirt, slip, and panties together and tore my panties. That night my mom happened to be home and I told her what happened and she told him not to do it again. However, I didn't tell her he tore my panties. I just changed them and threw the torn ones away. After that incident, she told him he couldn't come over when she wasn't home. I didn't like him after that and I tried my best to keep my distance because he was crazy. Nothing ever happened again.

Chapter 5

Desegregation

I attended P.S. 156 until the end of fourth grade. Then I was integrated into the white school. Of course, by then I was used to the white kids, and many of them were my friends. The school sent paperwork home for my mom to fill out. The paperwork was consent for me to integrate. As I recall, the paperwork had to be returned by a certain date. If the paperwork wasn't returned, we would be transferred to the white school anyway. I kept telling my mother she needed to sign the papers saying she didn't want me to be transferred. My mom didn't get the paperwork back in time and I was one of the many children that were integrated into the white school. I do believe now mom intentionally did not sign the papers. A Supreme Court decision held that racial segregation of children violated the Equal Protection Clause of the Fourteen Amendment. Maybe mom just didn't know how to explain it to me, but I do believe she refused to sign so that I could get a better education.

By this time, we had moved and I was a latchkey kid. The school was far enough away that I had to take a school bus to school. The bus would pick me up several blocks from my home.

The white school was in Sheepshead Bay. Wow, what a change. Nice school, nice teachers, but the work was extremely hard and I was not prepared. The teachers tried to work with me because I was really struggling. I was placed in special reading classes but would act out because I was not catching on.

At the end of the term, I got left back. I couldn't stop crying, just like when I first started school. My teacher told me if I went to summer school and passed the reading test I would get promoted to the next grade in September. I spent most of my summer in school, still had to repeat the fifth grade, and only had a couple of weeks to spend with my grandparents.

After summer school, I took the bus alone. I wasn't afraid because my sister and I had taken the trip several times now. It was routine. I had to change buses and was a little nervous about getting on the wrong bus, but I could hear my mom's voice telling me what to do. I followed her instructions, got on the second bus which took me to grandmas. God was with me on the journey and took me safely. As a matter of fact, God was always with us when we journeyed because we never had a problem, never missed a bus, and always made it safely to and from.

The day I arrived, my dad came to visit my sister because she was returning home in a few days. My dad always gave us $50.00 each. When he gave my sister her $50.00 she told him she was going to high school and needed more. He knew I had just arrived and asked me to give her my $50.00 and he would come back before I left to replace it. He didn't come back.

Chapter 6

The Trap

It was Sunday and my mother always made us go to church. If we were too sick to go to church, we couldn't go out so we went to Church most Sundays so we wouldn't miss our movie date. A group of us would go to the movies on Sunday if there wasn't an afternoon service. I sang in the choir. I loved to sing but I was no soloist. Our choir often visited other Churches. This Sunday after the morning service, my brother and I and some of the other children went with the preacher to another church. My brother had come to live with us permanently when he was four years old because his grandmother died. After the service the preacher took us back to our Church to pick up his wife before driving us home.

When we arrived, service was still going on so we headed back outside to play while we waited for his wife. The pastor stopped me and asked if I would go to the store to get him a soda.

As I was walking away, he said to me, "if I'm not upstairs, I will be downstairs in the basement." The words hit me hard and I wondered why. When I came back he was not upstairs so I went downstairs. The lighting was dim. I called out his name.

"Elder Bethea,"

He answered. "I'm here."

I started walking towards his voice and then in the dim lighting I saw him. I gave him his soda and headed back upstairs.

Then he gestured. "We can go out this way."

There was an exit door to the basement. As you walk out the door, the space was about the size of a small closet with steps that lead outside. I followed him to the door. He opened it and I headed out. The closet space was dark. When I headed out he said, "Wait a minute." I stopped. I thought he stopped me so he could put on a light so I could see. Instead, he pulled me back towards him. My backside was now touching his front. Before I realized what he was doing, he fondled my breast.

I recoiled.

"No."

He turned my head towards him and touched my lips with those big nasty wet lips. His lips were so big it felt like they covered my entire face. His kiss reminded me of King Kong's big wet ugly lips when he took the tiny women in his huge hand and slobbered on her. It felt so nasty and I knew it was wrong. At that moment, I heard a voice in my head.

Run.

I jerked loose from him and ran up the stairs. I found my brother.

"Let's go."

"But we are getting a ride," he protested.

"LET'S GO."

This time he knew I meant it.

As we were walking away the preacher comes up the stairs and had the nerve to say "good night" as if he had done nothing. I wanted to scream at him but instead grabbed my brother's hand and briskly walked away. What an evil, evil thing he did. My pastor!! I trusted him like a father, and he betrayed me. At that moment, I wished I was Supergirl. I would have given him a beating he would have never forgotten. He would have never touched another little girl. God was watching over me and I am so glad I paid attention to His voice. Many times we hear the voice but we don't listen. I can't imagine what else would have happened if I didn't listen when I heard the voice tell me to run.

My mom was not home when we arrived so I sat in the chair by the window and watched and waited. We had a living room chair in our bedroom that sat by the window. I couldn't stop wondering why he did it to me. Wondering what I did to cause it. It seemed like forever sitting there waiting for my mom to come home. Finally,

I heard the key in the door. By the time she got the door open, I was standing at the top of the stairs crying uncontrollably. She kept asking me what happened. I finally got myself together enough to tell her.

"He kissed me in the mouth, and touched my chest."

"Who?" she said.

"Elder Bethea."

"What??"

"Elder Bethea. He kissed me in the mouth, and touched my chest."

"Oh, my God."

After she finally calmed us both down, she called one of the deacons. He was not surprised. He said it had happened before to others and it was time something was done about it. He told my mother he would help us. He said he would have a discussion with the pastor.

I felt better because the deacon was going to help us and the preacher was not going to get away with the wrong he had done but the pain and anger lingered. It clouded my judgment and it was all I could think about. A couple of mornings later I was awakened out of my sleep to a conversation my mom was having on the telephone.

I could hear my mom saying "I know Deborah wouldn't say something like that if it wasn't true." I heard her say it several times. Then I heard her next say, "Why would Deborah lie?"

I couldn't hear what the person on the line was saying but I was getting angry because whoever it was they were calling me a liar. My mom finally got off the phone.

"Who was calling me a liar?"

"It was Sis Bethea," she answered. Sister Bethea was the preacher's wife.

"She wasn't even there. She was upstairs."

My mom tried to calm me down and told me to get ready for school.

When the deacon finally called back he said he had spoken with the preacher and he said I was lying. He said that he never touched me. He told the deacon to go ahead and take him to court and he would smear my name in court.

The deacon and my mom together decided it would be best not to put me through an ordeal like that because I was only ten years old. They didn't give me a say in the matter. No one was fighting for me. My grandparents hadn't fought to keep me. Now my mom wasn't fighting for my dignity. She was going to let this man get away with the wrong he had done. My anger is now raging inside and most days the pain is too much to bear. Everyone knew he did this to little girls but no one was willing or brave enough to stop him. Their solution was to leave the church. But that didn't ease my pain or anger. The news spread and I was so embarrassed. I kept playing the incident over and over in my head, trying to figure out what I had done to cause him to single me out because I didn't want it to happen again. Several families left the church but that didn't solve the problem and certainly did nothing for the pain that was raging inside of me. All I could think about was the fact that he kept preaching and molesting little girls. I wanted him out of the pulpit. I wanted him locked up. I wanted them to throw away the key so he could never get out and hurt other little girls. No telling what he would have done to me if I didn't listen to the voice in my head. I just kept playing that thought over and over. I also decided that since my mother let the preacher get away with what he had done, I had to take matters into my own hands. I made up my mind I would never be taken advantage of again.

Chapter 7

My New Assignment

My mom had to find a babysitter for my brother when he came to live with us because he was not school age. He was so bad. Even when my mother spanked him, it didn't do any good. My mother's friend took care of him and he was always doing something to scare her. I'm surprised she kept him. But she did. When he was in second grade he became my responsibility. My mom put him in the same school I was attending. He didn't like getting up and every morning was a hassle for my mom to get him up and dressed. Almost every morning we had to run for the bus because he would make us late. We even missed the bus several times because he wouldn't get up. I would be so angry because I would be up and ready. There was no reason for us to be late. He was such a brat.

We had an arrogant driver name Mr. Timpson. He was a little skinny, pop-eyed man. He was an angry man and always yelling. He had competition because I was just as angry or even more than him. He pretended he couldn't pronounce my name and called me 'Debarina.' Every time he said it the kids would laugh. They thought it was so funny.

One day I got so mad at him, I yelled back, "YOUR MOMMA NAME IS DEBRARINA."

He yelled back, "YOUR MOMMA," and we went back and forth yelling at each other.

By the time we got to school, he was so angry he jumped off the bus like a crazy man and started yelling to the bus attendant that I was disrespectful and he wanted me thrown off his bus. I tried to explain but she wouldn't listen because that was not the first time he had reported me. So I was suspended for a month. My mother was livid because we had free transportation, but now she would have to purchase two bus passes so my brother and I could get to school. I felt bad because I knew she couldn't afford it. But no one would listen to me. I kept telling them something was wrong with the driver.

After my suspension, I rode the bus and tried my best not to say anything to the driver because I didn't want another suspension. Then one day we were riding along when all of a sudden, a bottle fell out of the bus drivers back pants pocket. Before he could grab it and put it back I saw that it was a liquor bottle. I whispered to one of the kids what I saw but we both kept quiet. When we drove up to school, the driver got off first. When I got off I went right over to the bus attendant and showed her the bottle in his back pocket. She said she would handle it. We never saw that little skinny pop-eyed man again.

I knew something was wrong with him and kept telling them but no one listened until I showed them the liquor bottle in his back pocket.

I graduated at the end of the next school term and decided to attend the Junior High School with all my friends I had met at the integrated school. It was in the same neighborhood. By this time, I was acting out more and doing things I had no business doing. I started playing hooky from school with my friends. We would always go to someone's house or apartment. A couple of times we went to my friend Sheila's house. Her father had a bar in the basement full of all kinds of liquor. We would have a real party when we went there because we had plenty of free booze. We would drink, dance, get high and enjoy ourselves and flirt with the guys. One day some older guys showed up. I don't know who invited them or where they came from but they got mad because none of the girls wanted to have sex with them so we asked them to leave. They went outside and shot up in the air. We didn't even know they had a gun. Someone called the police but when they heard the sirens, they ran off. We were afraid the police were going to take us to jail for playing hooky but it was close to the end of the school day, so they never asked us why we were there. They were more focused on the guys with the gun and they left to look for them.

After that, we made sure if no one knew the guys, they were not allowed in.

Most days I got home before mom and would get the mail from the box. If you didn't show up at school they would mail a letter to your home. One day my mom got the mail before I got home. I lied and said it was a mistake and I was in school. She said she was going to call the office the next day to find out. I had a friend who worked in the office. When the call came in she was sent to my class to ask the teacher if I was in class. The teacher said no but my friend went back and said yes. I got away with it that time.

Then one night my mom gets a call from Sheila's mother. She told my mom that I had played hooky with Sheila and some of the other kids at her house and had drank up their liquor. My mom was livid. When she got off the phone she gave me a whipping I never forgot. I hated getting beat by her because she never knew when to stop. After the second time I got caught playing hooky, I gave it up. It was not worth the whippings my mother put on me.

Chapter 8

The Wedding

In my second year of Junior High School when I was fourteen, and my sister was eighteen, she got married. We didn't know she was getting married. She had said yes to her childhood sweetheart but didn't tell the family. Her best friend broke the news to my mom. Mom was hurt because my sister had received a scholarship for college for seamstress but decided to get married instead. Sewing came natural for her and the clothing she made was of professional quality. I was disappointed too because she was giving up on a great opportunity. Even though mom was disappointed, she started planning the wedding. My sister got married, November 29, 1969. It was Thanksgiving weekend and I was not happy. My mom cooked for days and all day Thanksgiving but we didn't have a Thanksgiving meal. All the food was for the wedding and she wouldn't let us touch it. I don't ever recall a Thanksgiving when we didn't have a big feast and I expressed my disappointment. Family was in town and they took my bed. Everywhere I tried to sleep someone came and I had to move. I ended up sleeping in the chair. However, it was a fabulous wedding. I was one of the bridesmaids. We were dressed in pink satin with maroon velvet tops and long pink satin jackets. The maid of honor's dress was blue satin. My sister made all the dresses. We looked great and of course my sister looked fabulous in her gown. A friend of my mom's made her gown. It was beautiful. The gown had a beautiful train that was so long the photographer wrapped it around in a big circle and had us standing on it.

After my sister moved out my relationship with my mom changed. Mom was missing my sister and complaining about her spending more time with her in-laws. I knew it bothered her because my sister was her world and now she had to share. I saw it as an opportunity to finally get some attention. My mom and I didn't have a mother-daughter bond. My grandmother took care of me during my formative years. My mother-daughter bond was with her. However, my mom knew how to get her way with me because she knew I needed her attention. She took this as an opportunity to draw me closer to her. She needed me now that my sister was gone and I needed her attention. Whenever she started her drama about my sister, I would tell her not to worry she had me. I kept the house clean, shopped, did the laundry, and whatever she needed me to do. I was getting some attention and that's all that mattered. I knew I was only a stand-in because whenever my sister came around I was almost invisible. I knew I was being used but the attention felt good.

We were both using each other. I used the fact that my sister left for the opportunity to move out of that dreadful middle spot and into the oldest child spot. She used me because she no longer had my sister to herself. My mom started raving about me and all I did for her. I loved hearing people say she was saying good things about me for a change. Even though she wanted it to come from my sister, she accepted it from me and I was getting some needed attention. I played the game and lived in my imaginary world. I had built myself up in my mother's eyes and she counted on me. Even though I knew she didn't love me the way she loved my sister, I was going to ride this train as long as I could. Wow, what if she had given me away...

My imaginary world was my security blanket. I lived in my imaginary world growing up when I didn't want to cope with a situation. Like when I couldn't watch what I wanted or didn't want to watch what everyone else was watching on TV, or when mom made me angry because she promised something and I didn't get it because my sister or brother would come up with something they just had to have. I would wrap myself in my security blanket and imagine I was an only child living in a big beautiful house with my rich parents.

I can't remember how old I was but I think I had made my sister mad. She blurted out "That's why mom was going to put you up for adoption."

I heard her words. They hurt, but I thought she was teasing because she was mad at me, but when I asked her if she was kidding she said:

"No, mom was going to put you up for adoption."

I still didn't believe her but she finally convinced me that it could be true. I marched in the room where mom was and told her what my sister said and asked,

"Is it true?"

She didn't answer right away.

I repeated myself. "Well? Is it true?"

Then she dropped her head.

When she dropped her head, I knew it was true. The hurt hit me in the chest like a ton of bricks.

Then she finally said, "Yes, it's true."

My heart was beating so fast now it was skipping beats. She went on to say that she had promised me to a well-to-do couple, but when I was born she couldn't go through with it. I felt myself getting sick to the stomach. I walked away feeling hurt, angry, and empty, because she had my brother after me who she loved dearly.

I continued to ask myself why she didn't want me, and if she didn't want me why did she keep me? Had she given me to the couple that wanted me I would have been loved, happy, and an only child? I can't remember if this is when my imaginary world started, but I know it embellished it because my mom said the couple that wanted me was well-off. I wished I had asked her more questions, but I lived with the pain. I never knew who they were but always thought how nice it would be to be an only child. I thought of them often growing up, especially those times when I was promised something but would have to wait because my sister or brother came up with something they needed. I didn't have the bond with my mother my sister and brother had. I always felt like the step child. I could only get her attention when the other two were not around. The relationship was nothing like the relationship she had with them and that hurt because all I could think about was she wanted to give me away, then had another child that she loved dearly.

I had a cousin that would say, "You're the stronger of the children and your mom knows that. She knows you can handle the disappointment of a broken promise better than your sister or brother." I was an adult before I understood what she meant.

Chapter 9

Saying Goodbye to Grandpa

Seven months after my sister got married, my grandfather died. We had gotten the news that he didn't have long. I was outside playing when my mom got the news. When I walked in the door and saw the look on her face I didn't have to ask. I could tell my mom had been crying. Then she looked at me and broke down in tears. My mother's nephew, the one that took me back to school many years ago was there and he tried to comfort her. When I heard the news, the pain started banging my chest like a hammer. I felt so angry at myself because I was rebellious and had stopped going to visit. I hadn't visited him for several years. I started crying and saying I wouldn't see him again. My mom said she would take me out of school to go to the funeral. The pain in my chest started to ease.

When mom got the call, she was in the middle of preparing dinner. She was too upset to finish so I told her I would do it. She was cooking collard greens and fried chicken. The greens had to be cleaned and she told me to look for worms, and make sure I get all the sand off

"Worms?"

"Yes, sometime they have worms so make sure you check them good."

"Ok."

Of course, I found a worm. I started yelling and threw the greens in the sink. I'd never cleaned greens before so I wasn't prepared for the worms. I knew I had to help my mom so I pulled myself together and finished cleaning the greens. Thank God that was the only worm I found. I didn't know a lot about cooking at age fourteen but kept asking questions and did my best. It wasn't mom's dinner but everyone sat down and ate with no complaints.

My mom, her nephew, and I drove to the funeral. We stopped in Philadelphia to pick up her niece and then traveled to Myrtle Beach. Lots of family came. Once again, I had nowhere to sleep. My grandmother said I could sleep with her but I told her I was too afraid to sleep in my grandfather's bed. She said she understood. Eventually, I went home with one of my aunts. On the day of the funeral we all met at grandma's house. Then we walked across the ditch to my cousin's house because that's where the highway was and where the cars were lined up. All of a sudden someone came rushing into the house and said the police were outside. From what

I could gather, my uncle had left Myrtle Beach years before because of some trouble. I don't know what it was because kids weren't allowed in grown up talk. Anyway, they thought the police might be there looking for my uncle and after some discussion, he agreed not to attend the funeral. I was sad because he had come many miles to pay his last respects and couldn't even attend the funeral. However, I do believe he attended the wake the night before.

At the funeral one of my grandfather's friends who was a preacher stood up to say a few words. He said he had talked with my grandfather before he passed and he had accepted Christ. I was relieved to know that one day I will see my grandpa again in Heaven. After the funeral we got back in the cars and headed for the cemetery. In the South, you sat down at the burial ground and watched them lower the coffin into the grown, fill the hole with dirt, and then arrange the flowers on the grave. Once they finished, they walked over to my grandma to ask if she was okay with the arrangement.

The soldiers did the 21-gun salute. I didn't know what the heck was going on or why they were shooting. I kept ducking each time they shot the rifles because I didn't want them to miss and shoot me. It was the first time I had seen a 21-gun salute unless it happened at

Uncle Coolidge's funeral and I was crying so hard I just don't remember. Later, I found out it was just a tribute and they were only shooting blanks.

One of the soldiers presented my grandma with the flag that had been on top of my grandfather's coffin. The day after the funeral, we traveled back to New York, dropped my cousin off in Pennsylvania and headed home.

My grandfather was seventy-five years old when he died. His birthday was September 19th, one day before mine. Every year since he died, I remember him and say "Happy birthday, granddaddy. I miss you so much."

We only had a couple of weeks left in school before summer vacation. The summer passed quickly. It's my last year of Junior High School. I had to make a decision on which High School to attend. In the 70's, most Junior High schools went to ninth grade, so I would be starting High School as a sophomore. I was happy I was not starting as a freshman because sometimes they were bullied. It was a busy year trying to finish up classes and deciding on a high school. The counselors didn't give black students the same help they gave the whites. We had to make a lot of decisions on our own. I always had the desire to help others. Growing up, if someone got hurt, there I was cleaning their wounds and bandaging them up so I thought I was destined to be a nurse. I applied and was accepted to Clara Barton School for Nursing. I was excited and couldn't wait to get to High School. I passed all my classes and graduated that June. Graduation was held at a theater in Flatbush. I can't remember much about the graduation. I was just happy I had passed my classes and was going to High School.

Chapter 10

Sixteen and Pregnant

That same summer I met Kenny, the man that would become my daughter's father. One night my good friend Mickey came to visit and he was with him. Mickey introduced us. Every time I looked his way he was staring at me. I was wondering who the hell he was and why he kept staring. I thought to myself, "He didn't know me and I don't think he wants to get to know me."

Later I found out he had been living in the South and had just returned to New York. His mom had sent him to live with family because he was misbehaving. Some of the girls we hung out with stopped by too. I could see there was something between him and one of them and assumed they were dating.

My sixteenth birthday was coming soon. Mickey said he and his girlfriend were going to take me out. I'm not sure exactly how the conversation continued but he said he had a surprise date for me. I had messed around with several guys but only considered one a boyfriend. I never thought I was pretty but I was at the age when my hormones were attacking me and my breast and hips where filling out to form a beautiful shape to go along with my big bow legs. I didn't notice my beauty. It had snuck on me, but the guys noticed. All of a sudden they started paying me some attention. It's funny, my first boyfriend and I argued all the time. I never suspected he liked me. Then one night he told me he liked me and wanted me to be his girlfriend. I was shocked, I didn't know what to say but he convinced me that he really liked me. We dated for a while but it never got too serious. I found out he was also dating another girl so I broke up with him. He wanted to go all the way, but I just wasn't ready. When Mickey showed up, Kenny was with him. When I saw him, I said, "Oh no, I'm not going out with him. He has a girlfriend."

I was upset with Mickey. They kept saying the girl liked him but she wasn't his girlfriend. After much convincing, I decided to go just because it was my birthday.

We were walking down Rockaway Avenue, laughing and talking and having a good time. Out of nowhere, there was the girl and her friend. She was livid. I played it cool. I felt like an innocent bystander caught up in a bad situation. I just wanted to go home. She confronted him.

He tried to downplay the fact that they weren't really dating but the way she carried on, it was clear they were a couple. I could tell by the look on her face she was hurt. She broke it off with him and angrily walked away. I was so mad with him, I didn't talk to him for a long time but he never gave up.

Somehow, he wiggled his way back into my life, though I should have never let him. We started dating and eventually going all the way. I remember it like it was yesterday. It was New Years Eve and we were out celebrating. After the party, we stopped by a friend's house. Her parents were not at home. We had all been drinking and celebrating a little too much. The next thing I know we are getting ready to have sex. I said, "Not without protection." He said he had a condom. After it was over, he looked at me with a blank look on his face. Right away, I knew something was wrong.

"The condom broke."

"Oh, shit."

We sat there for what seemed like hours. We both were afraid and didn't know what we would do if I was pregnant. The hammer started banging on my chest and I was angry at myself for finally giving in. We waited.

This was all I could think about every minute, every hour, of every day. January ended. February ended. The hammer was banging on my head and chest now, and I just couldn't stand the pain.

I contemplated having an abortion because I was so afraid my mother would give me one of her never-ending beatings. Both times she beat me; I thought she would never stop. I could see myself half dead, black and blue, and bloody before she stopped.

One Saturday while she was at work, I took her insurance card and went to the doctor's office. I told him my dilemma. He gave me some pills and said if they didn't work to come back. They didn't work.

The next Saturday, I was going to take the card and go back. My boyfriend knew what I was planning. He called me that morning before my mom went to work. My mom answered the phone. He asked to speak to me.

"It's for you. It's Kenny."

I took the phone. "Hello?"

"Hold on," he said. The next thing I hear was his mom's voice. I was so frightened, because the rumor was that she was crazy. My heart jumped out and was now in my lap.

She said, "Kenny told me you are pregnant, Deb. Please don't do anything that you will regret. We are here for you."

Mom was still in the room. I didn't know what to say except "Okay."

She said, "Okay. Here's Kenny."

I could hardly get any words out of my mouth because mom was still in the room. I was so angry with my boyfriend because he didn't let me know he was telling his mom. My head and heart were still pounding and I was trying to get my heart back in my chest. I wanted to beat the shit out of him.

When I hung up the phone, mom asked, "Why is he calling so early?"

"He wanted to talk about the party tonight."

"So early?"

"Yeah, he's on his way to work and didn't know if he would get a chance to call me."

She got up and got ready for work. After she left, I had all intentions of going to visit the doctor but I couldn't get the conversation with Kenny's mom out of my head. What should I do? Should I go and see the doctor? Should I tell mom I'm pregnant and let her beat me half to death?

I never left the house that day. I decided I had to find a way to tell my mom. The pounding in my head and chest just wouldn't stop.

How am I going to tell her? What will she do to me? Oh, Lord. Help me.

To my surprise, it happened that evening. She was in the kitchen cooking. She always prepared her Sunday dinner on Saturday evening. I walked in the kitchen, pulled out the chair from the table. I kneeled in the chair with my hands on either side of my chin and my elbows on the table.

Each month she would check with me to see if I had my menstrual. I had lied and said yes in January and February. I even used pads so she wouldn't get suspicious. As I'm kneeling in the chair with my hands on my chin and my elbows on the table, mom asks.

"Did you get your menstrual?"

It came out of nowhere like she had slapped me up side my head. I took a deep breath, and prepared for the knockout punch.

"It's not coming."

"What?"

"It's not coming," I repeated.

"How do you know?"

I took another deep breath. "I haven't seen it since December. I took your insurance card and went to the doctor. He gave me some pills to take for seven days and said to come back if it didn't come."

"Where did you go?"

"To the doctor's office on Stone Avenue."

"And they just let you use my card?"

"Yes."

"I'm disappointed in you, Deborah. I could tell the way you looked that you were pregnant. I never expected this from you."

She continued. "I gave you too much freedom for you to let this happen."

I stayed silent because I knew she was angry. She just kept talking.

"You will never amount to anything and you're just going to have baby after baby."

It felt like she had just stabbed me in my chest with a knife and the pounding in my chest felt like blood dripping down. I knew for her to say that she was really angry. I couldn't move. I was still kneeling in the chair with my elbows on the table and my hands on my chin, just waiting for the big blow. I felt like I had just lost my new best friend. All the work I had done to get her to pay me some attention had just gone down the drain.

I knew she was hurting because she stopped cooking and went in the room to lie down. She didn't say anything else to me that night and I left her alone. When I finally got the nerve to move from the table to finish getting ready for the party, I went into the room we shared and she was crying. I thought I should play it safe so I got my clothes and left the room. I felt so bad and angry with myself for going all the way.

About an hour later, my boyfriend came to pick me up, I opened the door.

"She knows."

"What did she say?"

"She's been in her room crying for a while."

He stood standing there with that 'deer in the headlights' look in his eyes.

"Let's go. I know she don't want to see either one of us now."

After we left the house I told him what she said, that I will never be good for anything and have baby after baby. He just looked at me.

"I'll show her. I will make something of myself."

The next day was Sunday. I was going with my sister and her church on a bus trip to visit another church. The phone rang. It was my sister calling to say what time they were picking me up. I heard my mom tell her,

"Deb's pregnant."

My sister was upset. She told my mom to tell me she wasn't taking me, and hung up. The pain in my chest was banging out of control. My head was about to explode. I didn't know what to do. I just laid there in bed. A few minutes later the phone rings again it was my sister calling back. She told mom to tell me to get dressed they would be picking me up. I don't know what changed her mind but I got dress and waited. I just knew she was going to add to my mom's hurtful comments when I got in the car but she didn't say a word. I tried to enjoy the day but kept waiting for the knockout punch. She never mentioned it. She didn't even seem to be angry with me. Maybe she felt sorry for me. Sixteen years old and pregnant. My life was ruined.

When my mother told my brother, he was upset, too. He told her to send me away until I had the baby. I think he was more embarrassed than anything because I was only sixteen. She told me what he said and that the pastor and his wife agreed. However, they wanted me to go away to have the baby because they wanted to adopt the baby. The pastor's wife couldn't have children and would take mine if I agreed. The pain in my head and chest is banging so hard now they are both about to burst wide open. I was glad mom said it was up to me, but if I decided to keep the baby, I would have to take care of it. She said she wouldn't be taking care of it because I laid down and made it and it was my responsibility to take care of it. I felt lost and alone. I had a big decision to make. How was I going to finish school? How was I going to take care of the baby? I was only sixteen, and couldn't even take care of myself but I didn't want to give her away, especially to my pastor and his wife who I see all the time.

My boyfriend's mom assured me that she would do everything she could to help. My girlfriend's mother said she would be there for me too. She was so strict with her own girls that I assumed she would be ashamed of me. To my surprise, she was supportive. She told her daughter she wanted to talk with me. I was so afraid because she was so strict. My head and heart is pounding even more now as I waited to hear more of the same talk as my mom. She looked me straight in the eyes and said.

"The first time is a mistake, and I will support you and do what I can to help. Just don't let it happen again."

"Okay."

I was in shock, but felt a little relieved. The fact that she was willing to give me a second chance just made me more determined not to make the same mistake again and to make something of my life. Now I had two people to prove myself to. I told my mom that I was going to keep my baby and I would get a job as soon as I could to take care of her.

Just before the end of the tenth-grade school term, I met with my guidance counselor to discuss my career plans. I told him I was pregnant and my baby was due at the end of September. I was six months pregnant but no one knew because I didn't show. I was in the nursing program and wanted to remain in it but knew I would be behind because I wouldn't be able to get back in school until November. He saw my determination to be a nurse and said he would work with me and allow me back into the program when I returned.

During the summer, I attended the school for unwed mothers. I stayed there until I had my baby.

It was a Wednesday afternoon, the day of my seventeenth birthday. I left school to go to my doctor's appointment. After the doctor examined me, she looked at me funny.

"Your blood pressure is extremely high. Are you feeling dizzy?"

"No." I shrugged. "I feel fine."

"I think you need to go to the hospital," she said. "I'm going to call for an ambulance."

In my rebellious voice I said, "No I'm not. I'm going home to get my mother."

I lived about four blocks from the health center. When the doctor realized that she wasn't going to convince me to go to the hospital without my mother, she gave me a note and told me to carry it in my hand in case I passed out.

The note said something like "Blood pressure is extremely high. Please take directly to the hospital." I put the letter in my purse and walked home. I had toxemia, which is extremely high blood pressure and swelling of the hands and feet. God was looking out for me because I made it safely home. I told my mom what the doctor said and gave her the letter. Then I told her I was going to take a shower, and change my clothes. When I was ready, she called a cab. By the time I got into the cab, I started feeling cramps. I couldn't get comfortable. My mom kept asking if I was alright. The cab driver must have thought I was in labor because he kept looking through the rearview mirror looking scared. He looked like he was so relieved to get us out of his cab. I went to the desk and gave the attendant the letter. She started processing me in. Once she finished processing me, she took me into the examine room to wait for the doctor. The doctor came in examined me and said, "You are going to have this baby before the night is over."

"No, I'm not."

Finally, they got me checked in and sent me to my room. To my surprise, one of the girls from the unwed mothers' school was my roommate. She had already delivered her baby. It was a boy.

My family and friends came to visit me during visiting hours. I was so uncomfortable and kept changing positions. I didn't say anything to anyone because I didn't want them worrying about me all night. By the time they were leaving, the pains started to get worse. I didn't think I was in labor so I just turned over and tried to go to sleep. The pains kept coming. About ten o'clock that night, I finally pressed the nurse call button. I told her I was having pain. She said,

"Okay, whenever you have a pain, turn on the light."

The next time I had a pain, I turned on the overhead light. I waited and waited but no one came. Finally, about eleven o'clock I pressed the call button again and told the nurse that I had turned on the light as directed but no one came. She explained that she meant for me to press the call button. Well, why didn't she just say that! Again, she said just press the button every time you have a pain. The pains kept coming closer and closer. I kept pressing the button until finally the nurse came in the room, checked me, and said she would be right back.

The pains kept coming and I kept pressing the call button. She finally returned with a bed and took me to the labor room. The pains were getting worse but I kept dealing with them. The nurse came in to prepare me for delivery. As I laid there in the labor room the pains kept coming. I began screaming.

The nurse kept checking on me but there was nothing she could do. Finally, a doctor came in to check on me. I was in terrible pain. The pain was so bad I grabbed his arm and just dug in with my nails.

"It's okay," he said, "just keep breathing."

The pains were coming closer and closer but my water had not broken. The doctor broke my water and they finally took me to the delivery room. It was a strange-looking place. I remember the table being round and not really looking like a table. It was stainless steel. This could have all been a dream but I would never know because I never went back into a delivery room again. I was so scared and all alone.

Once they moved me to the delivery table, I heard the doctor say, "When you see the baby's head, give her anesthesia," The next thing I knew, they were waking me up saying I had a baby girl. One of the nurses brought her over. I held her for a little while and then they took her to the nursery. I asked what time she was she born and they said 7:58am. I had been in labor all night.

They moved me back to the recovery room. The next thing I remember was the doctor coming in to check on me. He showed me the scratches on his arm. I apologized. He just smiled. I guess it wasn't the first time. Then he pressed on my stomach to make sure all the afterbirth had come out and more gushed out. He said he would send someone to clean me up but I laid there for hours before someone came. I guess they were changing shifts and someone forgot me because the relief nurse had a fit when she saw me. She cleaned me up right away. I wanted to eat because I was so hungry but they were feeding me intravenously because of the toxemia in my body. I asked if someone would call my mother. But no one called. I didn't see her until visiting hours that night because she worked during the day. She was surprised I had already delivered the baby. Since I was still in recovery, my mother was the only one that could visit because I was not married to my daughter's father. However, everyone was able to see the baby.

They didn't let me go back to my room until the next morning. I tried to take a shower but became dizzy and almost fell. I told the nurse. She scolded me for trying to take a shower without help. They brought my daughter to me to feed her. The first thing I did was check to see if she had all her fingers and toes. Then I checked the rest of her body. Her little ears were so dark. My mom said that meant she would be dark-skinned.

The next night, my boyfriend's mother came to the hospital to see baby Latisha. She didn't even ask for a paternity test. She just looked at the baby and said, "Yeah she's ours." She looked so much like them.

I stayed in the hospital ten days. The normal stay was five but the toxemia was still in my blood stream causing my blood pressure to remain elevated. The doctor said he could not release me until all the toxemia was out of my blood stream. After a couple of days, people stopped visiting. I was lonely. When visiting hours came I would be hoping someone would visit. On the ninth day,

I was lying in bed feeling sorry for myself and not even expecting any visitors. To my surprise, the youth pastor from my Church walks in. He saw the sadness on my face and asked,

"What's wrong?"

I told him I had been in the hospital nine days and I just wanted to go home.

"If you want to go home just tell God, and trust him," he said. "When do you want to go home?"

"Tomorrow."

"You will go home tomorrow if you trust God. When the doctor releases you, call me, and I will come and take you home." That is all I thought about the rest of the day. The youth pastor was my only visitor that day. He prayed with me, wrote his number on a piece of paper, and then he left.

The next morning, the nurse checked my blood pressure and took blood. This was the 6:00am routine every morning. Later the doctor came in looked at my chart, and said, "You are going home today." I jumped out of bed and started getting my clothes together. Then I pulled out the piece of paper with the youth pastor's number and called him. When I told him that I was discharged he started praising God. He and my mother picked me up. That was one of the happiest days of my life. I felt like I was being sprung from prison.

I was finally going home.

Chapter 11

Return to School

On my return to school, I went to the office to meet with my guidance counselor. To my surprise, his secretary said he passed away a couple of days before my return. Sadness fell over me. I had been assigned to a petite white woman who dressed well, every hair on her head was in place, and her clothes fit her like a glove. Her makeup matched her skin nicely. I liked her style. However, she was strict, and many of the students didn't like her.

When we met to discuss my classes, she said nursing was not an option because I was too far behind to catch up on the work and take care of a newborn. I said, "I can do it, just give me a chance." She kept saying it was not an option.

I begged her. I told her the promise the previous counselor made, but she kept saying it was not an option. She said she didn't want to put me in the program to watch me fail, and didn't know why my counselor would make a promise like that knowing how hard it would be to catch up and take care of a newborn. Pick another major, she said, but there was nothing else I wanted to do.

We went back and forth for what seemed like hours.

She gave me the list of options and told me to go home and think about them overnight. I was so upset because she was unwilling to give me a chance. I didn't want to go to school if I couldn't do nursing.

I talked to my mother about it but there was nothing she could do. I had made my bed and now I had to lie in it, as the old folks would say.

The next day I went back to visit her and tried one more time to convince her, but to no avail.

We went over the available options again, and she suggested marketing. After some thought, I settled for the marketing major. She gave me my schedule and I headed to class. I really had no interest in marketing but to my surprise, I loved it. I loved learning about the quality of clothes and role-playing scenes of selling my products. I was pretty good. I thought I could probably make a career out of it one day.

That semester was tough. I found myself sleeping through many of my classes because my daughter would keep me up most nights crying. One day my teacher woke me up. I had fallen to sleep in class. I was so embarrassed.

I became good friends with one of the girls who was in most of my classes. She sat next to me and would wake me up if I fell asleep. She was not in class the day the teacher woke me up.

At the end of the semester, I had to admit the counselor was right. I would have flunked out of the nursing program. Many nights I'd taken my daughter to the emergency room at Kings County hospital, but the doctors never found anything wrong. One even made the comment "she will have strong lungs." Later, after I thought about it, I cried my entire pregnancy. I believe that is what I taught her.

I decided since my daughter kept me up most nights I would go to night school the next semester. That worked out so much better. However, I could only take four classes so I went to summer school to make up some of the classes.

The next year, my daughter was sleeping through the night so I went back to day school because I wanted to graduate with my class in June. I still had classes to make up so I went to day school and night school. In order to graduate I had to take the reading and math test. I passed the math test but missed the reading test by a few points. They let me walk with my graduation class because I had passed all my classes, but I had to attend summer school again and retake the reading test. My mom was so happy to see my accomplishment. It made me feel good to see her happy again, and to hear her say she was proud of me.

The first night of summer school, the teacher gave us the reading test. We were told if we passed, we would get the passing grade, but still had to complete the class and retake the test to get the grade. Whichever grade was higher is the grade that would be submitted. I passed the test the first night. Even though I had to attend school the entire summer, it felt good knowing that I had passed and would get my diploma in September.

To my surprise, my diploma was dated June 1974. I thought it would be dated September because I had to go to summer school. They said it was dated June because I had completed and passed all my classes. However, the other student's diplomas were dated September 1974 and they were not happy. Those two years were two of the toughest years of my life.

In my final year of high school, I had a paid position in the office. I worked for the two guidance counselors, the petite white woman and an African American male. I got to know them well. Even though I had a baby, they had a lot of respect for me because they both saw my determination. When I discussed my plans with the male counselor to major in marketing, he said that was not a field easily open to African Americans and especially women. I valued his opinion because he had experience in the work world. He suggested instead of focusing on college right away, I go to a trade school, learn a trade, and get a job so I could take care of my daughter. He reminded me that she was not my mother's responsibility, and I could go to college later. Both counselors were strict but they gave me good advice.

I learned about a program at the Opportunities Industrialization Center (OIC), and contacted the school to complete the paperwork. They called me shortly afterwards to take the test. I signed up for computer programming because that's where the money was at the time. However, my score wasn't high enough for computer programming. The instructor said it was a passing score for refrigeration repair or key punch training. I didn't want to be in a class with all males because of my anger. I went with key punch because it paid well too.

Class was not starting until January of the next year so I worked for a temp agency for four months, at Bergdorf Goodman's stationary department. I loved the job and my boss. I worked hard and completed my assignments on-time, and she appreciated it.

The other temp was an older white woman. She

smoked and talked a lot. She didn't work as hard. When it was time to let one of us go, the boss fired her. She was not happy and voiced her opinion to me and the other lady that worked with us. We both just shrugged our shoulders but we all knew why she was fired. I believed she did too. I learned early in life that hard work pays off. I was able to keep the job until my keypunch program started.

Chapter 12

My Pain, Anger, and More Disappointment

I hated men, especially preachers. If a man became too close to me or looked at me in a way I thought was sexual, I'd lash out. I went through life thinking I was protecting myself. I cheated on men and thought nothing of it. It gave me satisfaction for the moment. I remember dating three guys at the same time.

One night I invited them all to a house party my club was hosting. It was ironic that they all showed up dressed in green suits. I couldn't believe they all had worn green suits. Was that a coincidence or was God trying to tell me something?

One was stuck in a card game his name was Bill so I knew I didn't have to worry about him. He gave me the keys to his car and asked me to hold them. I had been taking driving lessons and decided to sneak downstairs and take Bill's car for a joy ride. My brother and my friends were just as crazy as I was. They jumped in. We went for a ride. I had a carload. We drove around the block, stopped at the store, and headed back. When we got back the same spot was available.

Oh good, he'll never know we took it.

I started backing into the space and all of a sudden, the car shuts off. My brother and friends jumped out and tried to push the car into the space but somehow it ended up on an angle halfway on the sidewalk and halfway in the street. John, one of the other guys that I was dating, was just walking up in his green suit and tried to help. He suggested we get the owner of the car. I confessed I took it for a joy ride. He stood there shaking his head. I looked up and there was Bill's brother.

He said, "Where's Bill, and what happened to his car?"

"He's in a card game, and I drove it to the store. When I was backing up it shut off."

He didn't look like he believed my story.

"I'll wait with the car, go get him."

I went upstairs and told Bill it was an emergency. His brother needed to see him downstairs. I knew that was the only way to get him away from the game. As we were walking down the stairs I told him the real story. He said,

"Oh, that's okay. It shuts off sometimes."

When we got downstairs, and he saw his car he said,

"Oh, shit. What happened to my car?"

John and Bill's brother pushed the car and helped him get it parked. He worked on the car and finally got it started. This time, he put the keys in his pocket.

Back at the party, Bill went back to the card game.

I was with John who had just arrived. Since my club was hosting, it was understood that I had to be cordial to my invited guests. Just before John left, my third date Jerry showed up with his green suit. I excused myself to greet him. Out of the three, I liked Jerry the best.

Kenny showed up uninvited, and he had on a green suit, too. *God must be trying to tell me something.* I didn't have much to say to him because I didn't invite him. At that time, we were on the outs and he knew I was dating someone. He didn't know I was dating three at the same time, or maybe he did.

Kenny got the worst of my anger. I guess it was because I let him talk me into going all the way and I ended up pregnant and lost my mother's respect that I had worked so hard to earn. I would lash out at him and fight him like a man. I remember one time stabbing him in the hand with a fork just because he was trying to take food off my plate.

Another time, he stopped by uninvited. We were sitting at the kitchen table when he takes out pictures of his girlfriend to show to my daughter. I slapped him so hard I probably left my handprint on his face.

"Get out."

He got up and left acting as if he had done nothing wrong.

Once, he took me to a party at his cousin's house and I was slow dancing and kissing his cousin like he was my date. He tried to play it off as just a cousin. I didn't care who I hurt because I was hurting.

Another time during one of our break ups, he asked if he could stop by to see some mutual friends that were in town. He begged me to let him come. I finally said okay. After sitting around drinking and having a good time, he started saying he had to leave because his girlfriend was home waiting for him. My anger was raging inside but I ignored him. But he kept repeating it. It was as if he was trying to provoke me. After about the fourth time I lost it.

"GET THE HELL OUT."

But the fool wouldn't leave. I said it again.

He acted like he didn't understand what was wrong. Our mutual friends asked him to just leave. He still wouldn't leave so I jumped on him and started kicking his you-know-what. My best friend's husband tried to calm me down but the fool still wouldn't leave. Finally, my best friend's husband got him to leave. By now he had provoked me to rage. I followed him outside. One of the kids was standing there holding a bat.

I snatched the bat out of his hand, and went running after him. You talk about a fool run. He ran like he had super powers in his shoes. He jumped in his car just in time to save his ass. However, I guess he was so scared he couldn't get the car started. I busted out the driver's window first, "BANG." Then the front window. "BANG." Then the passenger window. "BANG." I was headed for the back window when the car sped off. I ran around that car with lighting speed.

After I calmed down, I realized I could have killed him. That frightened me. Had I killed him, my daughter would be without a mother or father. I didn't need her being angry too because I was angry enough for the both of us. After that incident, I vowed to God and to myself to never let anyone provoke me to rage again. Had he not jumped in his car when he did, he probably would have been a dead man.

After that incident, you think he would have moved on with his life. But he was a fool, he came back again, and again. Another time he ran into some mutual friends coming to my house. When I opened the door, he was with them. That could only mean he was heading to my house uninvited. Why else would he be in my neighborhood? He loved to brag and wanted us to go see his new apartment. He didn't stop until we all decided to go. He put on some music and served drinks. Then he and I drifted off to the bedroom. I went to use the bathroom before re-joining the group. I closed the door to use the toilet. As I sat there facing the closed door, there on the back of the door hung a little black dress. Anger immediately filled my chest. I thought, the bastard, he could have at least put the dress in the closet. I felt stupid and there was no way I was going to let him get away with disrespecting me. I also wanted his girlfriend to know just what kind of man she was dating. I found a razor in the bathroom cabinet and I cut up the back of that little black dress. Then I saw some nail polish in the cabinet and wrote *BITCH* on the front. Then I quietly rejoined the group.

When he rejoined the group, he couldn't find his watch. My friend's husband has slippery hands and he had eased the watch into his pocket. I knew he stole but my daughter's father was not aware of it. His wife begged him to give it back.

Finally, the watch just reappeared.

Another time my brother-in-law was driving me home, I spotted his car not far from my house. I didn't know why it was there. After my brother-in-law dropped me off, I went back to where I saw the car. I let the air out of every tire and bent both of his antennas.

Later I found out that the girl he was dating had moved into my neighborhood. This was the owner of the dress I cut up.

I tried several times to work things out with my daughter's father because she wanted us to be a family. In my heart, I knew I was just doing it for her. We broke up too many times for it to work. We would break up; get back together, just to break up again. He would just show up uninvited as if he had the right to. He often made the statement, "since he was my first he could always come home." So he thought. I realized he really didn't want to work things out. He just wanted to stop by and have sex whenever he felt the urge. I also think he was afraid of a permanent relationship because of the rage he saw in me. I knew it was no match made in Heaven and decided to move on. I knew it would break my daughter's heart but I had to move on with my life.

As I stated earlier, I liked Jerry the best and he won my heart, but not before I went on a trip to Ridgeland, SC. I rode with my brother-in-law and some of our other friends. It was a last minute decision. My sister and the children were already there. He was missing them and decided to surprise them for Christmas. So, I hopped in the car for the ride. We were there for a couple of days and went out partying each night.

One night I walked out into the yard and a man called my name. I turned to see who was calling me. The only person I saw was a man standing under the tree that I didn't know.

"How do you know my name?"

"I know everybody."

I just laughed and said, "Yeah right, I know some-one told you my name," and walked away.

Later that night at the club, I saw him again. He walked up to me and said,

"If you don't stop what you are doing someone is go-ing to kill you."

I looked up startled, and angry about what he said. It didn't take much to make me angry.

He said he knew I was dating several guys and I needed to stop what I was doing before someone killed me. I stood in awe, thinking who is this man? First I see him in the yard. Now at the club and he's telling me about my life. I had to get away from him. I had to wake up. This had to be a bad dream. Maybe God sent an an-gel from Heaven to warn me. I didn't know. It scared me something fierce. I had to wake up from this awful dream. Then I realized it was not a dream. I was in the club with my friends. I walked over to Mickey my good friend looking like someone had just took every word out of my mouth.

"What's wrong?"

"Not sure. My head is spinning. Who the hell is that man over there?"

"Oh, that's my cousin. He is gifted with the knowledge of *knowing*. He can tell you all about your life".

"Well, I don't need him to tell me all about my life."

When I got back from that trip I broke it off with everyone. I was taking my anger out on the men by cheating on them. It was giving me satisfaction. I needed to find another way to release my anger because it was so alive within me it was eating me up. What am I going to do? I didn't want to die but I needed the pain in my chest to stop hurting so badly.

I also used to fight to relieve my anger. If a male looked at me wrong I would be ready to fight. I don't recall having many fights with girls growing up but I had lots of fights with boys. One day I got into a fight with this big fat dude at school. His mother called my mother to complain about me scratching his face. I recall yelling "HE SHOULDN'T HAVE MESSED WITH ME AND I WOULDN'T HAVE SCRATCHED HIM." I even had a fight with a boy on the block that was later the head of a gang. I was always worried that he was going to have his gang beat me up. Thank God, he never did.

Whenever I got ready to fight, I would sneak in the house and put on my jeans. One day I came in and my mom could tell I was angry and figured I was up to something. She followed me outside and wouldn't let me fight.

Yes, it was a boy. After that, when I came in to put on my jeans my mother was always checking to make sure I wasn't sneaking out to fight. My brother was small for his age and the boys in the neighborhood would pick on him so I fought his friends too. They learned quickly not to mess with my brother or they would have to fight me. My brother finally had a growth spurt and all of a sudden, he became this big guy. I didn't have to worry about him any longer. When he had his fiftieth birthday party one of his friends came up to me and said "You know me. You were the one that use to fight all the time."

She knew me but I couldn't remember her.

Chapter 13

My Work Journey

I started the keypunch program in January. It came natural for me and I enjoyed it. I learned quickly and was one of the fastest in the class. There were four of us who adapted so successfully the instructor started sending us on interviews after just a couple of weeks. Different companies came to the school to administer tests. One of the companies was the Postal Service. I passed the test with flying colors. They called me for an interview, but they didn't hire me because I had no keypunch work experience.

I had an interview with the Corrections Department but passed it up because I didn't want to work in a jail with prisoners. I didn't want to lose my job if one of them touched me. I still had pain and anger deep within and would have lost it if one of the men touched me or said the wrong thing.

I went on another interview for New York City local tax returns and was hired. This was a seasonal job so I kept looking. About a month later, I was hired by the City of New York working in the Purchasing Department. I was the youngest there but was respected for my work quality. I enjoyed my job. It was fun except for the time I got into it with my boss. He made me mad and we had words. Thank God we didn't stay mad.

While working in the Purchasing department, I started seeing Jerry. He was so much fun. He would pick me up on Friday nights after I took a nap and we would hang out together. There was this song "Living for the Weekend." I loved that song. He would play it for me and I would dance, dance, dance. I loved to dance and started using dancing to release my anger. I could dance for hours. It took me to a happy place.

After working for the Purchasing Department for two and a half years, the Postal Service called me for another interview. This time they hired me because I had experience. I was torn. I wanted the job because it paid well and had great benefits, and I could finally go to college. But I wished I could stay with the job family I had come to know so well with the new salary. In the end, I decided to take the job with the increase in salary and benefits. They threw a big party for me. I cried and cried. I hated to leave a family I had grown to love. We worked so well together, but I had to move on.

When I told my daughter's father I had gotten the job with the Postal Service, his comment was "you make more than me and don't need my money". The little money he was giving me stopped. I didn't feel like I should have to beg a man to take care of his child, and did my best to take care of the two of us.

I started working at the Postal Service in July, 1977. I was excited. I would be working at the huge famous Post Office on 34th Street. It was like a dream that I never thought would come true. After the first interview, I had no idea they would call me back again. But there I was.

It's the largest Post Office in the country. It was 31 steps just to get to the first floor. The building is 22 feet above street level. At the top of the steps were these huge beautiful columns. They were so wide I couldn't even wrap my arms around one. Just above the columns read the famous lines: *Neither snow nor rain nor heat nor gloom of night stays these couriers from the swift completion of their appointed rounds.* Reading it sent chills down my spine. What dedication. Wow. The beautiful cream-colored building took up two full city blocks.

Inside, the lobby was just as beautiful with marble everywhere, and tall windows that gave the lobby lots of light, along with long hanging beautiful chandeliers that added to the light. This was the customer service area. Mail processing was on the second and third floors and our office was on the fourth floor.

My first night at work, the entire city went black. No power in the entire city. No lights anywhere. No trains running. I'm in the city and don't know how I'm going to get home. Jeffrey Dahmer was on the rampage at the time. This frightened me. One of the men on the job gave me a ride home. I didn't know this person. It was my first day on the job. He could have been Jeffrey Dahmer for all I knew but I took the chance because I didn't have any other choice. It was pitch dark when we arrived, and people were everywhere. He said, "I'll walk you to your door." Since it was dark, I agreed, but when we get to the door, this fool tried to kiss me. I said, "Oh no. Thanks for the ride but you cannot kiss me." He said good night and walked away.

The power was still out the next day. I called to see if I had to report to work. The supervisor said, "Yes." Since I was on probation, I went. I had to take four buses to get from Brooklyn to Manhattan. The same man drove me home again that night. By the next day, the power was back on and the subways were running.

I worked from 4:00pm to 12:30am. I didn't like the hours but I wanted to take advantage of the opportunity. I missed my old job and went back several times to meet with friends until I finally adjusted to my new job. It just wasn't the same. Working nights, six days on one day off, then five days on three days off was hard. My body clock just could not adjust. I gained weight and my sleep pattern was way off. It was not fun, but I had a goal. My goal was to work five years; quit, take the money I had vested, and go to college full time to get my Bachelor's degree in Nursing.

Things didn't work out the way I'd planned. God had other plans. I heard a man once say, "If you want to see God laugh, just make a plan."

By this time, the relationship with Jerry had gotten serious. One night he picked me up for the weekend and was looking sad. I asked, "What's wrong?"

He said someone had broken into his apartment. He left one of his friends there because he didn't feel comfortable leaving it. We drove back to his house. It was a mess. He was trying to straighten things up. He called me into the room and showed me an empty box. It was a ring box with three ring circles. I asked him to explain. He said he was going to propose to me Valentine's Day which was the next month. He had purchased the ring set for me and him. I thought it odd that he would buy a set with the ring for himself because I thought that was the women's responsibility. I was surprised and sad. He said as soon as he could afford to buy another set, we would get married. Since we were going to get married, I agreed to get an apartment with him. We found a nice place in Queens, NY and moved in that November.

Everything was going well at first. Then I started to see the real person: I had moved in with an alcoholic. I was so busy enjoying the time we spent together, I didn't even see it. He would drink sometimes until he passed out. Oh, my God, what have I got myself into?

When he got drunk, he would mentally abuse me. He would keep me up most of the night just talking stupid stuff. One night I fell asleep and all of a sudden I wake up wet. This fool poured a glass of water on my head. Then he would come back and make up, say sorry, and we would be a normal couple until the next time. Thank God, most times when he got drunk, he passed out. This went on for several months before I realized he was no longer talking about marriage. It didn't matter because I was not going to marry him unless he stopped drinking. I didn't see any sign of him quitting, so I started preparing myself to leave. I decided I would give it a year. If things didn't get better, I was out. He sold perfumes. I sold a lot for him at work. He said I could take half my profit. I would take half of the money for the perfume I sold before I gave him the money and then I would take another half when I gave it to him. I would also take most of the money out of his pocket when he passed out. I knew he wouldn't remember because he would be so drunk. I was banking all the money so when I got ready to move I would have enough money for my down payment. I had been praying for God to guide me to make the right decision. I didn't think I should waste anymore of my time, because I couldn't change a person that didn't want to be changed. I told him I was leaving. He begged me to stay but I told him I couldn't live like this. He said he would change. I told him I had been with him a year, and I didn't see any change. I just needed to go. I thank God that my daughter never saw him acting foolish. We were in our room when he would act up. It was sad because he was so lovable when he was not drunk. He loved us and we loved him but I just couldn't live this way. I had just started the day shift before I left.

When I moved out, I went back to my mom's place for a couple of months until I found a place.

I couldn't get my daughter into the school in my mom's neighborhood so I called her father's mother. She always supported me. She was glad to help out. We got her enrolled in the school near them. She stayed there during the week. I would pick her up on Friday after work and take her back on Sunday evenings. When my daughter's father found out, he called to see what he could do. I was cordial with him but I knew that was not where I wanted to go. But we kept in contact. Three months after moving to my mom's, I found an apartment.

The apartment was in the Bronx. My daughter's father lived in the Bronx on the other side of town. He thought I was moving to the Bronx because he lived there. I was moving because it was the better apartment of the ones I had looked at, and it had security. I rented a truck and two of my male friends moved me. He asked me if I wanted him to help. I said he could. When we drove up, there he was standing there directing traffic. He had already inquired with security and knew where we had to park. When we finished moving, I left him at the apartment and went with my friends to take the truck back. I told him I would be back later. I had no intentions of coming back until the next day. When we returned the truck, I told my friend to drop me off at my mom's house. Later that night he called my mom's house to see if I was there. I answered the phone and told him I was too tired to come back and would see him in the morning. The next day I took the train home. He was there waiting. When I got there, he had unpacked some of my things and put up the bed. I didn't have a living room set so I guess he put it up to have a place to sleep. He said he was going home to get some things that I might be able to use. When he returned, he had two plants and some other things. He said the plants represented the two women he was seeing and whichever one died was the one he would end the relationship with. I told him I was not good with plants but he left them anyway. Of course, in no time they both died and I threw them out. He also gave me one hundred dollars and told me to put it away for emergencies. I thanked him and shortly afterwards he left.

It felt so good to be alone in my apartment. The first week I spent time enrolling my daughter in school and finding a babysitter. A friend of mine lived there. Her friend who was a building security guard recommended a babysitter. Since she came recommended, I didn't ask a lot of questions. She was very nice and my daughter loved her. She had two boys. One evening my daughter was bending over like she was hurting. When I asked her what was wrong, she said the babysitters' youngest son had kicked her in her private parts. I was livid but I waited until the next morning. I took the day off. I went to her house that morning and told her what my daughter said. She beat the little boy right in front of us. She said it wouldn't happen again. I told her I was not comfortable letting my daughter stay and she wouldn't be coming back. She said she understood and we left on friendly terms. Anytime I ran into her we were always friendly with each other. I found another babysitter that week. She had two boys as well. I explained the situation I had just taken my daughter out of and she said that would not be a problem with her boys and I had no need to worry.

A couple of weeks later my daughter's father stopped by. He said he had received an eviction notice. I told him that he had to get the money together because he couldn't stay at my place. I still had the hundred dollars he had given me but I didn't offer it to him. I felt like the whole thing was a set up to see if he had a chance with me. I wondered then if maybe one of the plants had my name on it. Years later, he was still in the same apartment. Even though he said he was there for me, he really wasn't. He thought he was going to be able to get back in. When he realized that wasn't possible, he wouldn't help. I called him once and asked if he could help pay our daughter's tuition because I was short. He said he didn't have it. He said, "I'm getting married, and you need to find your daughter a father."

Wow, what a low blow. I gave him some choice words and told him not to worry. We would be fine.

My daughter liked her new babysitter they were very nice people and I was glad. They all went to the same school. They watched out for her. However, the school system in the neighborhood was not to my satisfaction. I decided to keep the job and put my daughter in private school. The private school had an after-school program. My daughter stayed at the program until I got off from work. Later, I put her in the Boys and Girls Club after school program. It was free, and had lots of after school activities. My daughter loved the program.

Since I decided not to quit my job and put my daughter in private school, I could only afford college part-time. After being out of high school for four years,

I finally started a two-year community college program. It was overwhelming. I started to suffer with migraine headaches. My doctor sent me to a specialist. The specialist had me lay out my schedule. When he saw all I was doing, he said, it was no wonder I suffered with migraines. He said I needed to give something up. Well, I was a single parent and I didn't live near family, the only thing I could really give up was school, there was no way I wanted to give that up. The doctor said if I didn't give up school I had to learn how to use my time more wisely or the migraines would not go away. He suggested things like using a crock pot to cook meals. Back in the day, there were no microwaves. A good friend brought me a crock pot. I would put things like beef and potatoes in the pot leave it cooking all day and when I'd open the door, the food would smell so good. I learned how to use my crock pot for many meals. I also brought a toaster oven and taught my daughter how to use it. She mostly used it to heat up meals I had already prepared, make cheese toast or any little concoctions she could think of. I kept making adjustments because I was determined to succeed. Each week, I made a list of activities for the week and we made a plan of how to accomplish them. Sunday was the only day I could rest. I rested Sunday mornings. Then I would get my chores done for the week in the afternoon. I would cook several meals, and wash and prepare our clothes. In the evening, we did homework. After many adjustments, the migraines stopped.

I majored in accounting. I don't know why I chose accounting over nursing. However, the first semester I enrolled in a psychology class. I enjoyed it so much. The next semester, I switched my major to psychology. I would leave work, pick up my daughter, take her home to the babysitter, and head off to class. Often times, I took her to class with me. I sat in the back of the room so I could help her with homework. We would go to the library on Saturdays and while I did research, she would do homework or read books. We lived in the library. I remember one day we were talking and my daughter asked where babies come from. I tried to fluff it off but she was not buying it so I said, "get your coat, we are going to the library." We walked to the library. When we arrived, I went to the desk and told the librarian my dilemma. She said, "Oh, that's easy" and gave us the Chicken Book. It was a book about how chickens were born. We sat down. I started reading the book and all of a sudden it became clear to her. She understood that it takes a sperm of a male and the egg of a female to make a baby that was enough for the time being. I told her we could discuss it more when she was older.

Thank God for the Chicken Book!

Chapter 14

How I Met My Husband

As I said earlier, I was working days now. The Keypunch room was across from the vending and copy machine that everyone on the floor used. This brought lots of traffic outside our room. There were certain guys that would always be hanging around the area. Some were nuisance, and I would hate to run into them. I remember one guy saying that I was stuck up because I wouldn't give him a play. Then one day I went out to the vending machine to get a drink and this guy was there getting a drink that I had never seen before.

He turned and there I was standing behind him waiting to get my drink

When he turned, we locked eyes.

He had a puzzled look on his face.

At last, he finally spoke. "Hi."

"Hello."

He paused a beat, then said "You look familiar."

Oh, no. The pick-up line.

I put my guard up."Don't think I know you."

"I've definitely seen you somewhere before."

This guy is handsome. But I'm not falling for this line.

"Did you go to Jefferson High School?"

"Yes."

His face brightened."I thought you looked familiar. My name is Joe."

"I'm Deborah."

"Nice to meet you."

"Nice to meet you too."

I moved up to the vending machine, as I moved to the machine, he walked away. I put the coins in the slot, selected my drink, picked it up when it fell in the tray, and then went back to work.

A couple of weeks later, I ran into Joe again.

"So what year did you graduate?"

"I graduated from Clara Barton High School 1974."

He looked puzzled. "I thought you said you went to Jefferson?"

"I did. I went there for night school to make up some classes."

"Oh. Maybe I know you from somewhere else then."

"I don't know where it could be."

"You look familiar."

I shrugged my shoulders

Then he asked,"Would you go to lunch with me?"

"No."

"You're turning down a free lunch?"

I gave him a look that said *I know you just didn't say what I think you said.*

Then, I said with attitude, "Yes. I'm turning down A FREE LUNCH," and walked away.

I was so angry. My face probably turned red. I had experienced the same response from a drunk man when I worked as a Christmas casual years before. This man was drunk and demanding I go to lunch with him. I said no thank you nicely and tried to walk away.

"Well excuse me. You're turning down a free lunch."

I turned around and put my hands on my hips. "Yes, excuse you. I'm turning down a free lunch."

Just then, my supervisor walked up. I don't know what would have happened if he hadn't, because this angry woman was ready to defend herself. He was drunk so I probably could have whipped him easily.

After that, I kept my distance from Joe for many years because he reminded me of that encounter. I don't think I could have whipped Joe, but by the time I finished with him he would have thought I did.

Computer terminals were just becoming popular, and would eventually phase out keypunch. The payroll department posted several computer terminal jobs. The keypunch operators were encouraged to apply because we were fast on the keyboard. Several of the operators applied. We were all promoted. We were fast on the keyboard, but we had to be taught the system and the work. It was overwhelming, so much to learn. I don't think they were ready for us. The first two weeks we were all seated together. The supervisors came over and introduced themselves. We were given odd jobs to do. Then after the two weeks, we were dispersed into different units. Two other ladies and I went to the filing unit. I was disgusted. I applied for the computer terminal job. But all day long the three of us sat and put documents in social security order. Then we had to go to the file room and file the work in folders. Filing required standing, and many times we ended up with paper cuts. This was not what I signed up for. The supervisor said the jobs would be rotated but couldn't tell us when. Our team leader was a woman that cussed about everything. She even cussed us. However, it wasn't long before we bonded with her. Under all the cussing, she was a sweet person. She loved crocheting, and made us lots of things. She also stuck up for us and kept the unwanted guys away.

Years later, I received a call that Jerry had been hit by a train and was in the hospital in the Bronx. The next day I went to the hospital to see him. When I arrived, his sister was there with a man and a lady. I talked to his sister to find out what happened. I found out that he was on the train platform waiting for the train. He got too close when the train was entering the station and was hit. The first thing I thought he must have been drunk. Later I found out that the woman he was living with was on drugs. She had run up a tab with the dealer. They came looking for him for payment and beat him badly. I finally asked his sister about the lady and man. The man was his best friend. The lady was his wife.

"Did you say wife?"

"Yes, that's his wife. His daughter is downstairs."

"His wife."

"Yes."

I was stunned. "He told me they were divorced."

"No, they never divorced … He left her after the baby was born but they never divorced."

What a slap in the face. I couldn't wait for him to wake up to give him a piece of my mind. Jerry told me he only married the woman to give the baby his name and the marriage had been annulled. I dated him for at least two years, and never met this best friend or heard the truth about his wife. It was no wonder he acted so foolish. He knew he couldn't marry me. I wondered now if there were ever any rings in the empty box. I went to the hospital every chance I could, just waiting for him to wake up. I was the last one to visit him. It was Christmas

Eve. I was sitting there still waiting for him to wake up so I could tell him off. The nurse came in and asked;

"Where's his family?"

"I believe they are all planning to come tomorrow."

She looked at me and shook her head. The next morning, I received the call that Jerry had passed away. I never got the chance to give him a piece of my mind. I attended his funeral to say my last goodbye. I was still angry with him for not telling me the truth but not mad enough to stay away.

The thought of him being married stayed on my mind. Then one day I received a letter from the apartment complex we shared. The letter stated that we owed them back rent. I called them up and told them I moved out years ago. They told me that my name was never taken off the lease. I also told them that Jerry was dead. They said I would have to send a copy of my lease and a copy of Jerry's death certificate to clear the matter. Immediately, I called Jerry's sister. She told me the wife had the death certificate. We had become close while visiting Jerry and had exchanged numbers. Since I knew who his wife was, I just assumed she knew who I was. However, when I called to ask for a copy of the death certificate she was puzzled and wanted to know why I needed it. I told her about the letter I received. She still sounded puzzled. I told her we lived together for a year.

"You didn't know?"

"No."

"Oh I'm sorry, I just assumed his sister told you."

"No, she didn't. Now tell me again why you need the death certificate?"

"When I left Jerry, my name was never taken off the lease now they are trying to charge me for back rent. I need to send a copy of my new lease and Jerry's death certificate to clear up the matter. I'm sorry I thought you knew we lived together."

"No, I assumed you guys had dated, but I didn't know you lived together."

"I'm sorry you had to find out this way."

"It's okay. What's your address? I will put a copy in the mail."

It was an awkward moment. Before that conversation, we had exchanged numbers and said we would keep in touch but that was the last conversion we shared. She sent the copy of the death certificate and I took care of the matter.

One night I had a dream about Jerry I saw him pass though fire. When he came out of the fire, he was charcoal black. He said something to me but when I woke up I couldn't remember what he said. I interpreted the dream to mean that he was apologizing and thanking me for all the prayers I sent up to heaven for him as he laid in the hospital bed. I also interpreted it to mean he had come to know God while in the hospital bed and that he had accepted Him as his Lord and Savior. If this is true, I will get a chance to ask him why he didn't tell me the truth when I see him in heaven.

After Jerry died, I started thinking about what my grandmother said about being angry with my dad. The kids had been asking about him and I thought it was time they meet him. That summer, my sister and I took the kids to Myrtle Beach on vacation.

Since he was married, my grandmother didn't like us calling his house. She told us to always have a man call and tell him we were in town. Well, Ms. Rebellious decided to call. His wife answered the phone. I asked to speak to him by name. She said he was not home and asked if I wanted to leave a message. I said I would call back later. My grandmother was not happy about what I had done. I was starting to feel bad about it too so I had my male cousin call back. My dad poured concrete for a living. He owned his own concrete business.

He asked to speak to my father.

"Hello Ed. The girls are in town and want to see you before they go back."

"Okay. I will be there in the morning to pour the concrete." I guess his wife was sitting in the room.

I didn't believe he was coming, but at least I tried. To my surprise, I received a call the next morning informing me that the man was at my aunt's house to pour the concrete. It was my cousin on the phone. I thought she was joking. I finally realized she was serious. I dressed and took my daughter to meet her grandfather. My sister and her children were already there. I was still angry with him but glad he didn't disappoint the kids. He tried to give us the usual one hundred dollars. My sister told him we didn't want his money. Said the children had been asking about their grandfather and we just wanted them to meet him. He wouldn't take the money back. He said to split it between the three children.

After my father's wife died, he and mom started seeing each other again. By this time, he had lost his sight to glaucoma. He told us the reason he was blind was because he didn't trust doctors and didn't get there in time to save his sight. I guess I understand why.

One day we all were at my mom's house. He asked to speak with my sister and I privately. We went in my mom's bedroom and shut the door. He started apologizing for not being a father to us and the tears started flowing. I finally got a chance to tell him how angry I was that he didn't come back with my money. He apologized and tried to give me fifty dollars. I wouldn't take it. We told him to give it to our mother because she struggled to raise us as a single mom. He apologized again and more tears flowed. After that, anytime he saw my mother he would give her money. He had three boys with his wife. We had heard that his middle, son had died many years ago. The youngest one lived with him. The older one lived in Washington, DC. We wanted to meet them. He said the one that lived with him would probably be okay with meeting us but didn't think the oldest one would like the idea.

One night, we drove him home and his youngest son was there. He introduced us. He warmed up to us right away. He started teasing me saying I wasn't his sister because I looked too mean. He did wood carvings and showed us some of his work. It was amazing. He said he would carve our names for us and asked for the correct spelling, but before he completed the work, he died. This was about a month after we met him.

My dad later told us that he had started on our carvings and was excited about it. We never found any sign of the work. My dad was legally blind and the only colors he could see were black and white. He had the cabinets in his kitchen painted white with black handles so he could see them. If my brother made the carvings he couldn't see them. I just assumed that the oldest brother threw them out. My dad said our oldest brother was mean and that we probably wouldn't like him. We said we still wanted to meet him.

We were home for the 4th of July one year and so was he. He agreed to meet us. We drove 25 miles to meet him. When we got there, he was next door. My dad said they had gotten into an argument and he changed his mind. He was right next door and probably saw the car drive up. I was disappointed because he wasted our time. My dad told us that we had another sister and another brother from other women. He said our sister had another sister and although the mother said she was his daughter, he said she was not his child. He told us where our sister worked but didn't seem to know exactly where our brother was. I prayed that one day we would meet.

After Jerry died, my good friend Miles, that had earlier brought me the crock pot, started visiting on a regular basis. One day he told me that he really liked me and wanted to be more than friends. He said he had always wanted to be more than friends. At the time, I was not seeing anyone. I agreed to give it a try. After dating for a while, he asked me to marry him. He was the one that moved me from Jerry's apartment to my mom's house, and then moved me to the Bronx. We had been good friends since high school and lived in the same neighborhood. He was someone I thought I knew, so I said yes. We went to the jewelry store and I picked out a ring. Then we went to mom's house to tell her the good news. It was a Saturday evening and mom was cooking her Sunday dinner. We told her our news, but she didn't look happy. She said she was shocked because she said it came out of nowhere. She knew we were friends but didn't think it was that serious. When he asked her for my hand in marriage, she was slow to say yes but eventually said yes.

After we became engaged he started acting different. He usually called each night and would come over on the weekends. The calls became less and less. Sometimes he would call maybe once a week. The weekend visits became less and less. I remember going to look at the place for the reception. He had a fit because he thought it was too expensive. I had never seen him act like that before about money. I was shocked. When we returned home, he was still carrying on about the cost. "The Cordon Bleu" was a beautiful elegant place. He carried on so terrible I told him that we could look for another place. Shortly after that he stopped coming at all. He would call every once in a blue moon. I always prayed for God to give me guidance. I didn't want to marry him or anyone else if he wasn't the one. Then one day he called. I told him that I was breaking it off because I didn't think either one of us was ready. He sounded so relieved and asked if we could be friends. I told him I needed some space and didn't want to see him.

Shortly after we broke up, I ran into a mutual friend.

He told me that Miles had no intentions of marrying me. It was all based on a bet. He said that because I was vulnerable Miles knew he could win the bet. I was so angry. I said to myself, if I ever see him again I am going to walk up to him and punch him in the face. He was a train conductor in New York City. Every time I rode the subway I looked for him so I could punch him. I never saw the bastard again. After that I didn't date for a while. Whenever a guy would ask me out, I would say I needed time because I had just gotten out of a bad relationship.

I was finally moved to a unit where I could work on the computer. The work was broken down by social security range. I was responsible for all work in my range. I had a lot to learn. My new team leader only wanted to show me once how to do a job and expected me to get it. If I came back with questions, she would say "I already explained that" and sigh when I told her to explain it again.

I worked with her for about three years, and then was moved to the Headquarters unit. I wasn't supposed to go to that unit. My supervisor had fought to get me the garnishments job. Another woman didn't like where she was placed and convinced the manager to switch her to garnishments. When my supervisor found out, she was livid. She came out of the meeting walking fast. I could tell she was upset.

"DEBBIE! COME HERE"

I walked up to her desk and said, "Mrs. Walker," do you have to yell?"

"Sit down." She pointed her finger in my face. "I fought to get that garnishment job for you, but Rosy has talked the manager into giving it to her because she didn't like the job they gave her. You need to go right into his office and demand your job. Go. Now."

I walked down to the manager's office.

When I knocked, the manager looked up as if he knew why I was there.

I expressed my disappointment with what he did and told him I wanted it corrected.

"Let me see what I can do and I'll get back to you," he relented.

I left the office. About an hour later, he called me back to his office and asked if I would take the job in the Headquarters unit.

I was so excited. This unit was where all the top bosses work was processed. It was better than garnishments work. I would be learning everything. Mrs. Walker was happy too, and said it only happened because I stood up for myself.

The work was hard but I had a great female team leader who was knowledgeable of the work. There was a male worker on the team too. He was young, fun, and crazy. We called him White Boy. We all got along great together. About a year later, our team leader left and we got another team leader.

She was nice and always helpful. We had a great relationship, too. One day I encountered a job I had never seen before. I asked my team leader for help. She said I needed to ask Joe Warren because he was the guru. I put the work aside. I did not want to ask Joe "Free Lunch" Warren for anything. I asked others for help but everyone referred me to Joe. About two weeks later, my team leader received a call about the case and asked for the status. I admitted I hadn't started it yet.

"You need to get it done right away. You've had it too long." She was right.

After getting over myself, I walked over to Joe's desk. "Can you teach me how to do 'Leave Buy Backs?'"

He smiled. "Sure, when do you want to start?"

I dropped my head embarrassed. "Now. I've had it for a while and they are checking on the status. Elaine said I have to get it done ASAP."

"I'll come over after break."

He finally came over and showed me the basics. He taught me enough to get me started. He was very thorough. Then he said, "When you have questions just stop by my desk."

I had several questions before I finished the case. He explained the work in a way I understood. He didn't seem to get upset that I kept asking questions. After I completed the case, he reviewed it and corrected my errors, and gave me more tips. I thanked him again.

He didn't' seem like the same person all those years ago that said, "What, you're turning down a free lunch?" Was it all a dream?

I had other cases and would go to him when I needed help. I didn't get them often so it took a while to learn plus they were all so different. My team leader and everyone else were right. Joe knew his work.

After that, I started speaking to him when I saw him. Besides, it would have been rude after he took time out of his busy schedule to teach me. Then the Headquarters group merged with Joe's unit. We started talking more and more.

Since he wore a wedding band, I had to ask. "Are you married?"

"Yes."

"I hope that didn't sound strange. So many players wear wedding bands that aren't married."

"Oh, I'm not a player."

Hmm. Maybe he's an okay guy.

"I'm married, and have a son and two daughters. My son is the oldest."

Maybe I was wrong about him.

I finally told him why I didn't talk to him. He said that was not something he would say, and that I had gotten him mixed up with someone else. I told him it pissed me off because it happened with a drunk man when I worked as a Christmas casual at the Post Office. Again he said, "That's not something I would say."

Well, maybe I was wrong. Could it have possibly been one of the jerks that were always hanging out there? I will never know.

By now I was dating again. I had met this guy on the train one morning. The doors of the train were closing, and he jumped through the door just as it closed. I was standing near the door not expecting anyone else to get on when all of a sudden I was bumped by his heavy briefcase. I turned around and there was this tall nice looking guy in a business suit carrying a silver steel briefcase. I had an angry look on my face, and said, "Ouch."

He started apologizing profusely. I stared at him and rolled my eyes. He apologized again. I just ignored him. Again, he said, "I'm so sorry, my name is Richard." He kept on until he got me to talk. We talked until I got to my stop. He jumped off at the same stop and said he would like to take me out sometime, asking if he could have my phone number.

I said, "No, give me yours, and I'll call you."

I called him several times before I decided to go out with him or give him my number. He was the sound man for shows and concerts. He invited me to one of his concerts. The man he was doing the sound for called him Shaheed. I had heard several other people say that name but didn't connect it to him because I thought his name was Richard.

I looked at him with a puzzled look on my face, and he quickly said, "I'll explain later."

We stopped at a restaurant after the show.

"I'm Muslim. I knew you wouldn't talk to me if I told you."

"Yes, you are right. You lied to me."

"I know, and I'm sorry."

"Sorry. I don't want to be Muslim."

"I don't want you to. I really like you, and I know you wouldn't talk to me if I had told you."

"Take me home. I need some time to think."

The next day at work I was still upset. Joe asked what was wrong.

"I have been dating this guy for six months, and just found out he is Muslim. I really liked the guy, but he lied to me. I don't think I can ever trust him. He said just take time to think it through before making a decision."

"What is there to think about? He lied."

"Yes, he did, because he knew that was his only chance. Well, I don't want to be Muslim."

"Yes, and you made him aware of that right?"

"Yeah."

"Well, just think about it before you make a decision."

"Yeah, thanks."

I dated Shaheed another couple of months. Then he started making comments about the way I dressed. Saying I was showing too much of my body. I told him we could continue to be friends but I no longer wanted to date him. He agreed, but the calls got less and less until they finally stopped.

This was in 1985, just before we moved into the new building. The company had rented space in a building at 1250 Broadway. After they sign the lease, they found out it was not the safest neighborhood. Someone tried to snatch the purse of one of the women from the first group that moved in. Then it happened to another woman, and this time they snatched her purse. The manager met with us to let us know what happened. He suggested the women get a buddy partner. Another lady and I asked Joe to be our buddy partner because we knew he was a security guard, and he said yes. Joe would go with us to lunch and then walk us to the train station after work. On payday, he would walk with us to cash our check them walk us to the subway.

Joe always came to work with a nice pair of slacks, shirt, and tie. One Monday he showed up without his tie.

We both looked at him and wanted to know where his tie was.

"I forgot it."

The next day Joe came to work again without a tie. We didn't say anything to him.

The third day he came without a tie again, and I said, "Now, this is the third day you come up in here without a tie. What's up?"

He smiled. That's the other reason I kept away from him. He was always smiling. I assumed he was a lady's man.

Usually, the three of us were always together, but this day the other lady didn't come in. Joe and I headed out to Long John Silver's for lunch. While we were having lunch, he said,

"I left my wife. That's the reason I don't have any ties."

He said he'd packed his bag and was staying at his mother's, and had forgotten his ties. I was shocked. He never once mentioned that they were having problems. I told him he should try to work it out because of the kids. He said he would try. I also told him that I would go with him after work to pick out some ties. If I noticed it everyone else noticed it too.

After work, we went and picked out five ties, and the next day he started looking himself again.

After several months, Joe said that he had given a lot of thought to what I said and had decided he was not going back. After he made the decision that he was not going back, our relationship changed. We became best friends. We both decided we would be friends and see where it goes. Besides, I was still concerned that he would go back because of the kids. I enjoyed our friendship. I wasn't sure I was ready to enter into another relationship after all I had been through. Besides, I had a rule to never date a guy I worked with. But I started to really like what I saw in Joe and the icing on the cake was when I said to one the guys that I thought Joe Warren was a player, and he said, "No, not Joe Warren, you've got the wrong guy."

I decided that if he wasn't going back to his wife, I would give him a chance. We finally started dating. I can't believe I had broken my golden rule never to date a guy I worked with.

When the other women found out he had left his wife, they started interfering. One of the women told him that I slept with my supervisor and that's how I got promoted. He was upset and confronted me. I told him she made it up because she was jealous. This was the same lady that took my garnishment job. He realized the women were trying to break us up. Women started hanging around his desk, just to get on my nerves. I think the supervisor realized what was happening and moved me to another unit. One night we left work and two of the women from the office followed us. I guess they were jealous because they wanted him too. Who wouldn't want a good man?

After we were in the new building for two years, we received letters that our job was relocating to Minnesota. This was a very stressful time for everyone. We all had a big decision to make. I had to decide if I was going with my job or try to find a job in New York. My family was telling me not to go. My daughter didn't want to go. I also had fourteen credits left to graduate.

I started applying for jobs just in case I decided not to go. I even talked with my pastor. He said he didn't believe God wanted me to go and I should be able to find a job in New York.

But after weighing the pros and cons, I decided it would be best to go with my job. I had worked for the company ten years, and would lose my tenure if I started over with another company. I was offered a job with the department that was staying but when I inquired about the success of that department I was told it wouldn't be long before that department would be moving as well. I decided if they were going to close that department in a couple of years, I might as well go with my job. Of course, my daughter was not happy. She did everything she could to stay. I couldn't leave her with anyone because she is such a strong-willed person and outspoken. I told her she was my responsibility and she had to go.

Besides, after what her father had said, even though he later apologized, I didn't think it would be a good idea to leave her with him. At the time, she didn't know her father had told me to find her a father. She didn't even know he never paid child support. I didn't want to turn her against her "dead-beat dad." I wanted her to learn who he was for herself. I knew that would come as she matured.

After much thought, I told Joe I was going with the job, and understood if he didn't want to go. He said he had given it a lot of thought too, and decided because of his tenure as well, he was going with the job. I was happy because we had developed a great friendship and relationship.

In January, 1987, we found ourselves in Minnesota. My daughter was in her first year of high school when we moved. It was the middle of the school year. I think the timing was purposely done so we wouldn't follow our job. Also, it was Minnesota in the dead of winter. What other reason would they move us in the middle of the winter and middle of a school year? My daughter talked me into allowing her go to public school because she was tired of wearing a uniform. I checked out the school system and decided to take the chance. I figured it was the least I could do since she didn't want to go.

In New York, she was an "A" and "B" student and was on the honor roll. Because of her grades, she was placed in advance classes. She was the only African American in most of her classes, and was teased because of her New York accent. She also had problems with the other African American students. They treated her like she thought she was better than them. In order to fit in with the children of color, she "dumb down," and by the end of the school year she was bringing home "C" grades. I knew my daughter was not a "C" student and figured out right away what was happening. She kept saying the advanced classes were too hard. I told her she could take regular classes the next year.

That June, Joe and I went to the Justice of the Peace and were married. We drove back to New York afterwards, and my sister had a reception for us at her home. It was nice, and good to see so many friends. After the reception, we drove to Myrtle Beach, because I wanted my grandmother to meet the man I married. We stayed a couple of days and then returned to Minnesota.

I left my daughter in New York for the summer, and she returned at the end of the summer.

When school started back, I kept my promise to let her take regular classes. She was excited because she was with more children of color. I thought things were going well. Then, one day I received a call from the school. They said they'd found an empty pill bottle on her and believed she was trying to kill herself, that she was very upset and crying uncontrollably. The school called 911 and were taking her to the hospital. They wanted me to meet them there.

Terrified, I called my husband, and off we went to the hospital. By the time we arrived, they had calmed her down. She told them she had only taken two pills because she had menstrual cramps. I confirmed this, telling them I give her two pills for her menstrual because her cramps are really bad. I don't think they believed us, because we were assigned a social worker, who met with us to discuss our family life. After the meeting, the social worker dismissed our case. He said he didn't see anything wrong with our family life. The reason she was so upset was because some boy she liked broke up with her for another girl. I wanted to shake some sense into her. This incident cost me $500 because our insurance didn't cover the ambulance ride.

My daughter soon went to a concert with some friends and didn't come back when she was supposed to. I gave her a couple of licks she would never forget. She said she didn't want to live with me anymore. She said she wanted to go live with her dad.

I was angry with her. "Fine. Go. "

She called him and he told her to wait until the end of the school term. Of course, that day never came. He made some excuse why she couldn't come. He kept putting it off and it never happened.

She kept saying as soon as she finished high school she was going back to New York. She was planning to stay with her father. She applied for several colleges in New York but was not accepted because of her grades. I knew she wasn't going to be accepted with "C" grades and told her so but she applied anyway. She attended a community college in Minnesota for a year. However, she was still not making good grades.

The next year, I refused to pay so she didn't go back for a while. She was still trying to move back to New York to live with her father. She spent Christmas with him and they ended up getting into a big fight. He was so upset he accused her of being angry like her mom. He didn't speak to her for years. She came back home after her vacation and decided to stay in Minnesota.

I didn't apply to college right away because of the residency requirements: you have to live in the state for a year or pay higher tuition. I waited because I didn't have money to spare. However, five months after moving to Minnesota, I married my best friend. Research says best friends make the best marriages because you need love and friendship to make a marriage work. There must be some truth to the research because my husband and I have been happily married for 30 years. My daughter has a better relationship with him than with her father. I guess I made her father happy because I found her not just a father but a wonderful father.

When I finally registered, I found out that no matter how many credits I had, or how close I was to graduating, I had to take thirty credits in the state of Minnesota. I felt like I was going backwards but didn't let that deter me. I paid for my classes the first year, and my job paid the rest. I got my two-year degree. After that, I was hungry for more. I started working on my bachelor's degree. I took two classes each semester. That was all I could handle with a full-time job, and a new husband.

When I relocated to Minnesota, I worked in the payroll department as a payroll specialist. The next level was a payroll specialist senior, then a supervisor. I was determined to move up. I applied for training and positions when they were available. I didn't socialize much after work with my co-workers. One day one of my co-workers said I would never move up in the organization because I didn't fraternize with the crowd.

I remember saying to him "What God has in store for me no one can take away," and walked away.

I didn't let his comment discourage me. I kept applying for training and jobs. They kept saying I wasn't qualified. I filed several complaints against the department because they were not promoting employees from New York. The director said they needed to bring us up to the level to compete. I told him he didn't need to bring me up to the level to compete, just give me an opportunity to show my experience. After they saw that I wasn't going to drop my complaints, they privately settled. If I mentioned the settlement to anyone it would be null and void. I kept it to myself. After the settlement, I applied and was accepted into their supervisory program.

After completing the program and a two-year assignment I was promoted to payroll supervisor. I went from payroll specialist directly to payroll supervisor.

I had completed a supervisory program and assignment in New York, but they downplayed any training or experience we received in New York. Instead of sitting back and complaining, I took action. Since I went directly into supervision, it showed that my New York training and experience counted for something.

Chapter 15

My Awakening

After being in the position a couple of years, things took a turn for the worse. I had a great relationship with the manager because I did my work well. One day a new supervisor was hired. Once she joined the team, things were never the same. She was the devil in a dress. The manager went from respecting me and my work to always finding fault. I realized this supervisor was filling her head with lies. I knew then my season in payroll was over and it was time to move on. I started searching for other jobs.

One day, I was on my way to a funeral of a co-worker. I was looking pretty down when I bumped into the manager of the Information Technology (IT) department. He was the former director whom I had developed a good relationship. He asked, "Is everything alright? Can I do anything to help?" The words just flew out of my mouth.

I said, "If you have a job for me."

"What type of job?"

"A supervisory position."

"Okay, I will see what I can do."

I didn't think any more about it. A week later,

I received a call from the manager of the Customer Support department in IT. She said, "I was told you were looking for a supervisory opportunity." I was shocked. I couldn't speak for a second. Finally, I managed to say, "Huh?" She repeated it. I quickly said, "oh yeah!" We discussed a start date. We both agreed we had to give my manager a two-week notice. She asked if I wanted her to call. I said it would be better if she heard it from me. I was so excited. I went directly to her office. She was not happy. She said I could only go if someone covered my position that she didn't have to pay. That could only be another supervisor, and every supervisor had heavy workloads. I walked out of her office disappointed. I walked down to a supervisor's office who was a friend. I told her my dilemma. Without hesitation, she said, "I'll cover for you." This would double her workload, but she said she didn't care because she didn't want me to miss out on such a great opportunity.

I thanked her, gave her a great big hug, and I walked back to my manager's office to tell her the good news. Again, she was not happy. I thought she would be happy to see me leave since she had so many complaints about everything I did. However, she said she needed to talk with the other supervisor first, and would get back to me. The supervisor told her she could handle the additional work load. She was upset, but had no excuse for not letting me go. Two weeks later, I started the assignment. My hours were 6:00am-2:30pm. The detail lasted three months. The Customer Support manager wanted to extend my assignment, but my manager said no. About a month after I returned, the position was posted as a permanent job. I applied. I was interviewed and believed I had a good chance because I had worked in the position for three months and the manager wanted to keep me. A month passed, and I started wondering what was taking so long. I started having thoughts that I was not getting the job.

I was looking for a Church home at the time. I attended three churches, and heard the same message, "Wait on the Lord." Each time I felt like God was talking directly to me as we often do when we have been out of the Church for a while. I started to prepare myself for "sorry you didn't get the job." One day, I was sitting at my desk and the phone rings.

"Hello."

"Hi, Deborah, this is Mary can you come to my office?"

"Yes, I'll be right there."

I took a deep breath, prayed, and asked God to give me the strength for "sorry you didn't get the job." Then, I walked over to the manager's office. After some small talk, she said, "sorry you didn't get the job. I selected someone with more experience." She said it was a tough decision because we were both good candidates and if she had another position, she would hire both of us.

I said, "no problem, you said you selected the best qualified." Then I asked, "Who did you select?" When she told me, I couldn't help but wonder how she had more experience. Then she said the selectee had experience with some of the equipment. I pondered the thought; why would a supervisor need experience with the equipment? A supervisor job is to supervise and manage the work. It's the employees' job to have experience on the equipment because they are the ones who resolve customer's problems. But I kept the thought to myself. I told her I was going to stop by her desk and congratulate her. She looked surprised and said,

"Oh, that's mighty big of you."

"Well you said she was the best qualified, so I don't have a problem with that."

She gave me a hug, and I left her office.

I went and congratulated Martha. She looked shocked. Her face turned red. I told her if she needed help don't hesitate to ask. She thanked me. A couple of days later, she asked if we could meet to discuss questions she had. She wanted pointers on how to handle the employees. A large majority of the employees had relocated, and there was a culture difference. Since I had relocated from New York, I found it easier to interact with them. I told her to be herself and listen to what they have to say.

I couldn't stop thinking about the message from God, and I resolved to wait on Him. I trusted him because He made an impossible situation possible. When I went to congratulate the supervisor, she shared that she had applied for the same assignment and the manager refused to let her go. She said she was shocked to find out I was going. The only reason I could go and she couldn't was because God had answered my prayer.

I was alone when I got the news about the job. My husband was back in New York spending time with his daughter that had been in a car accident. When I told him he was in disbelief, and was sorry that he wasn't there to comfort me. I assured him I was okay. I realized God needed me alone with Him so that He could work on me.

Chapter 16

My Encounter with God

My husband and I had not settled on a Church home. We attended several churches, but still had not settled on one. Every year we listed it as one of our resolutions. Finding a church had been weighing heavily on my heart. I had prayed and asked God to send me a good husband, and I would find a Church home and serve Him. I knew I had to make good on my promise because God had answered my prayer. Besides, I was tired of the situation at work, and felt like things were going wrong because I had not lived up to my promise.

One day I was thinking about how hard I was working and accomplishing nothing. I said to the Lord that I had tried everything I knew and things were just getting worse, so I was putting my life in His hands. I was brought up to believe I had to do my best first before God would help. That was not true, and I missed out on God's guidance for many years. By trying to do it all myself, I found myself under unnecessary stress and carrying a heavy load. I didn't know all I had to do was give it to the Lord. After putting my life in God's hands, my life changed. I had an encounter with God. My guess is that

God was tired of me straddling the fence and wanted me to trust Him.

My husband and I were getting ready for vacation. We were going to a family reunion on his mother's side. We were excited. We came home from work and were preparing to leave later that night when we received a call that his baby daughter had been hit by a car. We threw our bags into the car and headed to New York. When we got there, she was stable, but had serious injuries. After being there several days, we decided to attend the reunion and return afterwards.

On the way to the reunion, my husband started to get tired and stopped to let me drive. As soon as I started driving, I started feeling light-headed. I tried to keep driving so my husband could get some rest. All of a sudden, a car in front of me hit a stick that was lying in the road. It flipped over and landed in front of us. There was no way I could get out of the way because there were cars on either side. I ran over it. Just before I ran over it, I saw the nail lying upward and was sure it stuck in my tire on the passenger side. Then it flipped over again and rolled on. I told my husband. He said we would check the tire the next time we stopped. I was still feeling light-headed. My husband said we would stop at a rest stop which was coming up in a couple of miles, and he would take the wheel. I felt bad because I had only driven a short distance and he didn't have a chance to rest.

We stopped and changed drivers, getting back in the car without checking the tire. Again, we said we would check it the next time we stopped. We drove about ten miles when all of a sudden, we came to a complete stop. The traffic was backed up, and we both wondered what had happened so quickly. As we crept along for about five miles, we saw a terrible accident. People were running around in disarray. There were bodies and body parts' laying everywhere and a semi-truck in the ditch. The man looked dead. People in other cars were cross ways in the ditch. They looked dead too. A man was running around taking pulses. All I could say was "Oh, my God!" over and over. All I could think about had I kept driving, it could have been us in that terrible accident had I not stopped. God was looking out for us.

We stopped several more times, but each time, we forgot to check the tire. We kept saying, "We'll check it next time."

We finally stopped at a gas station around midnight. My husband called to check on his daughter. While he was talking, he turned around and saw the tire was completely flat. He went inside to ask if anyone could fix it. The man told him to go across the railroad tracks and he would see a repair shop on the left. My husband put air in the tire and we headed across the tracks. We didn't see anything that looked like a repair shop. We saw a garage and decided to turn around because we thought it was the wrong place. As we backed up a man came out in overalls with a long beard looking like a hillbilly. I was scared because we were in the Deep South headed towards Alabama. My husband said, "You wait here I will see if he knows where the shop is." As he got out of the van another man came out. I grabbed our long "six D" battery flashlight. I was ready to help if necessary.

"Can I help you?" My husband asked if he knew where he could get a flat fixed. He said we were at the right place. I started praying because it didn't look like a repair shop to me. The man jacked the car up with me in it. I'm thinking how will I help my husband? I decided I would jump down if I had to help him. I kept my eyes on them, and the flashlight in my hand. He took the tire off, put it in water, and found the hole. Plugged it up, put the wheel back on, and put the car down. My husband asked "How much?"

"Five dollars."

I wasn't sure I heard him correctly. When my husband got back in the car, I asked, "Did he say five dollars?"

"Yes."

I was in awe and spellbound. I couldn't believe it only cost five dollars. It could have cost a lot more because it was midnight and we didn't have choices. I thanked God for keeping us safe. We drove on through the night, and arrived in Alabama the next morning. It was too early to check into the hotel so we went to my husband's uncle's house. We took a shower and changed clothes. We went to the hotel to check in around noon. We were so tired we laid down and fell asleep with the TV on. Three hours later, I was awakened by a news reporter reporting on a terrible accident in Maryland. I sat straight up in bed. It was the accident we had witnessed the previous day. The reporter said a woman lost control of her car, ran in front of a semi-truck and caused the semi to derail and hit other cars before landing in the ditch. At least six people died in the accident. I was spellbound again. What if we hadn't stopped to change drivers? We could have been one of the six that died. I thanked God for watching over us.

Later that summer, we attended my husband's father's family reunion. I was talking with the wife of one of his cousins and she said she had just accepted God in her life. We talked so long that we were late for the banquet. During our talk, she said God had taken away the taste of beer. I had been having self-talk and saying it was time to keep the promise I made to God. I loved beer. I drank it like it was water, so I wanted to give it up before I went back to church. Listening to her talked about how God had taken the taste of beer from her, I'm thinking that I had two beers left in my cooler and was going to drink them.

As we were traveling back home I was thinking about the conversation I had with the wife of my husband's cousin, and all of a sudden it hit me. I had had an encounter with God!! First, the accident with my husband's daughter there was no way she could have lived if God's angel wasn't there protecting her. When the car hit her, she was on a three or four lane highway with extremely high traffic. But by the grace of God, she landed on the edge of the sidewalk, and not in the middle of the traffic. I'm sure God's angels protected her. Then traveling to the reunion, I kept feeling light-headed, and had to pull over. God's angels were again watching over us. Then even with the nail in the tire, we drove about 500 miles before the tire became totally flat. I know God's angels were watching over us. As flat as that tire was, we should have been dead at the speed we were traveling. This was the second time in one day that God had kept us safe. It was midnight. What repair shop is opened that time of night? God's angels watching over us again. Just think about how they were dressed! I told my husband that if we turned around and went back there would be nothing there.

Then God bonded me with my husband's cousin's wife. How ironic that we both loved beer. He sent her to tell me that just as He took the taste away from her He would do the same for me. He was showing me that He was taking care of me. All I needed to do was trust Him. Sometimes you have to see before you believe.

I had told God I was putting my life in His hands, but still didn't trust Him completely. I guess God got tired of me not trusting Him, so He showed me. He knows everything about us, and He knows I am a visual person. Things make sense to me if I see the picture. Although God was working with me the entire summer, it took the trip back from the second reunion to put it all together. God is awesome and He surely knows how to get your attention.

After we returned from the reunion, my husband went back to check on his daughter. I was home alone for about a week. I couldn't stop thinking about all God had done, and I wanted to keep my promise. I asked God to take the love of beer from me. I no longer wanted to love beer or anything more than God. By the time my husband returned, I had drunk my last beer. I told him about my promise to God, and that I was going to find a Church and keep my promise. To my surprise, he said, "Okay." I realized he had received the message from his cousin's wife too. Later, I tried to drink a beer at my husband retirement party, but it tasted like water. I did not enjoy it.

Chapter 17

Now Watch God Work

About a month after my interview with the Customer Support manager, I received a call from her. She asked if I would come to her office. I had a feeling it was about a position, because one of the supervisors told me he was leaving. But I would have never expected what happened next. I walked over to her office. She said,

"I have another position, and it's yours if you want it. You don't need to reapply because it's only been a month."

I didn't have to reapply?

She said the hours were 11:00am-7:30pm. I told her I wanted the job but was attending classes two nights a week working on my bachelors' degree and would need to adjust my schedule on those nights. I also needed to know if she would pick up the cost from the Payroll department for my classes. She said she didn't know. She said she would have to look into it later. I told her I was too close to graduating so that would need to be considered before I take the job. She said she would get back to me. I called my husband to tell him about the offer. I also told him I wasn't sure I was going to take it and why. He reminded me that I only had four classes left to graduate and maybe I should share that information with her.

No sooner than I got off the phone with my husband, one of the supervisors from the IT department came over to congratulate me. I explained my dilemma. She said, "Oh don't worry about that. She will work with you."

Anyway, I took my husband's advice. The next day, I went back to her office and explained that I only had four classes left to graduate. Before I could explain further, she agreed to my terms.

I was speechless for a moment because it didn't sound promising the day before. I thanked her, and said I would take the job. What a difference a day makes even a few minutes when you trust God with your life.

Learning a new job and keeping up with my school work was not easy. However, the good thing about the hours, I got to sleep in the mornings after I attended classes. The constant adjusting of my schedule was getting tiresome, but I knew it wouldn't be long. I asked the Lord to continue to strengthen me for the journey.

It was getting close to graduation day and the devil tried his best to frighten me. I was sitting in the office talking with the other two supervisors. I mentioned I had a few more papers to turn in. The same supervisor who got hired before me said something to the effect that she remembered a friend getting all the way to the end, and not graduating. I can't remember what else she said, but what I heard was not to get my hopes up because anything could happen. I said to her "that won't be me," and ended the conversation. I thought that was a terrible thing to say, and negative as well. But it only encouraged me to work harder to complete my assignments. The devil can use anybody. He has no shame.

When it was time to graduate, all my paperwork was completed, and I walked down the aisle feeling so proud of my accomplishments. I started thinking about where I had come from: I was considered a statistic because I was a teen mom; my mother said I would never be good for anything and I would just have baby after baby. I had to leave my family, and deal with my daughter's attitude because she didn't want to be in Minnesota. I had to deal with all the attitudes at work, while missing my family. I'm glad God made me a strong will-person, because I would have given up. When I graduated with my bachelor's degree I thought back to the time my cousin took me back to class in 1st grade and said, "You better stay." After that, it seemed I couldn't get enough.

After I received my bachelor's degree, I took a year off. Then I went back to get my master's degree. When I turned in my paperwork, the manager said, "I'm going to pay for your classes up front. You have shown you are serious about your education."

The paperwork had to be approved in advance.

After you passed each class with a "C" grade or better, the company reimbursed you. I had planned to use my credit card, and when the job reimbursed me pay if off. However, I was glad she decided to pay up front because sometimes something else would come up and I would have to use the money. That was a blessing I wasn't expecting. There was God looking out for me again.

One day I was in my manager's office for my yearly evaluation. She said, "I'm impressed with your leadership skills and want to provide training to further help you develop."

I asked about a multicultural leadership course one of the other supervisors had attended. She thought it was an excellent idea because it focused on African Americans in leadership. She signed me up right away. The instructor was a psychology major and a drill sergeant. I learned so much about myself during the course.

Chapter 18

God's Boot Camp

The first week in class, the instructor made a comment about me not having a problem getting a man because of my beautiful body. The men in the class were making comments in agreement with her. It made me uncomfortable and angry and I shut down. However, I realized it was something I had to deal with if I was going to be successful in leadership because I worked mostly with men. Before the next session, I called the instructor and told her about my molestation. She asked me if I would be willing to share my story with the class at the next session. I said, "Yes."

As I shared my story, I started to get emotional. The instructor said it was because I was still angry. She said it was time to release the anger so I could move on with my life. I didn't realize I was still angry about the molestation because I always talked about it. I thought because I talked about it, I was over it.

She said, "let's role play." She put a chair in front of me, and said, "Pretend the preacher is sitting there and tell him how you feel about what he did." I started telling him how I felt but I was not into the role play.

The instructor rolled up a newspaper and said, "Make believe this is a bat, and hit him." I took the rolled-up newspaper and started hitting the chair, but I still was not into it. Then she rolled up another newspaper and said, "Let me help you." She started beating the chair. All of a sudden, the role play took life. I could vision him sitting there and I started wailing him with the bat. I couldn't stop. I didn't stop until I wore myself out. When I finally stopped, tears were streaming down my face. I just plopped down in my chair. I looked around the room, and at least three of the students were crying. The instructor said there were a few of us that had things in common. The tears made the connection that something sexual had happened to them too.

After I calmed down, we discussed what happened. The instructor helped me realize my problem with men in authority. My unconscious mind was my protector. Anytime a man in authority got too close, my unconscious mind alerted me. However, I didn't understand what was happening until the roleplay exercise. Whenever my unconscious alerted me, fear would overcome me. I had promised myself I would never let anyone take advantage of me again, and my unconscious mind was only warning me. I didn't realize how the molestation had affected me mentally. It was a rude awakening. I just sat there and I felt so free. I had finally resolved a problem that had haunted me for years. The instructor said even though I was aware of the problem, it wouldn't go away overnight, but I would start to heal now that I was aware of the unconscious alerts.

I was dumbfounded when I got home. I sat quietly for most of the evening, unless my husband asked a question. It took until the next morning to discuss the experience with my husband.

I took many leadership classes after that, but none compared. God was truly working in my life. I was grateful that I finally turned my life over to Him.

Chapter 19

God's Blessings

I remember walking down the hall to my office one day, and thanking God for all His blessings. I was feeling good about all He had done. Thinking about how He helped me out of many bad situations.

Once, before I had the revelation talking to my boss' manager Rachael about her sudden change of attitude. She said I was angry. I lashed out, "I'm tired of white people saying I'm angry. Whenever we express ourselves we are labeled as angry." Well, little did I know I *was* angry.

I was walking and reflecting and thanking God.

Thank you, Lord, for your many blessings. Now Lord, I'm not complaining but it sure would be nice to work 9-5 again. But Lord, I'm NOT complaining.

Later that day, my manager Mary called and asked me to come to her office. As I walked down the hall, I asked, "Lord what it is now?"

She is going to offer you her job.

Then I said, like Abraham and Sarah in the Bible when God told Abraham that Sarah would have a baby in her old age. "That can't be true. She didn't get a promotion."

But God doesn't lie. As I got closer to her office I prepared myself for what God had revealed to me. I sat down.

"George and I have been discussing your leadership skills and believe you would be the best person to fill my position." I just looked at her.

She had to repeat herself because I just sat there in shock. "You don't have to answer right away. Think about it and come talk with me tomorrow."

I couldn't wait to call my husband. Since I trusted God, I trusted that this would somehow turn into a permanent nine to five job.

When I told my husband, he said, "What is there to think about? Take it!" Joe always supports me, and never objected to me advancing above him. He truly loves me, and I truly love him.

The next day I went back and told my manger I would be glad to step into her shoes. She made the announcement to the staff. She chose me over Martha, the supervisor she hired first because she had more experience. What a blessing to "Wait on the Lord."

Martha was not happy that she was not being offered the opportunity. She kept complaining about not being given the opportunity but would not ask the manager. I got tired of her complaining to me and asked the secretary to schedule a meeting for the two to meet.

Once the meeting started, they realized I had set it up. The manager agreed to give her an opportunity. After I was in the assignment three months, we rotated positions. Her hours were also 9-5.

During the time, she was on the detail, the head manager George called a stand-up meeting. We were all wondering why. He announced that Mary was leaving the company. She had taken a job with Land O'Lakes. The only word I could get out was "Wow!" She never mentioned anything about leaving. However, I should have known when they decided I would be best to handle her position. George was impressed with the way I managed. After Martha worked the detail three months, I went back and worked until I was permanently promoted into the position. I enjoyed working with George. He always challenged me to think outside the box. Because of it, I ran a smooth operation.

When I was promoted to the position, we were installing a new payroll system. We worked with the best of the payroll team to learn. With any new system, there will be problems until all the kinks are worked out. My job was to gather data on problems that happened each day, and put it in a memo in layman's terms for the Vice President and his staff. I was told never be late getting the information to the Vice President. After sending the notices for several weeks, the VP replied and said I was doing a great job keeping them informed. He then said he was going to be in town in a couple of weeks and wanted to meet me. I replied immediately. I said I was glad he found the information helpful, but unfortunately, I would be out of town, but looked forward to meeting him on a future visit.

George was tough. He challenged me and pushed me hard. Shortly afterwards George retired. After George retired, we had several different managers. Gary became the head manager of both California and the Minnesota Customer Support Help Desk. Before him we had been under different management and we did things differently. Gary's goal was to standardize the two offices so whichever office you called you got the same answers. This was no easy task.

He assigned me to oversee the standardization. My biggest challenge was to get the two offices to agree on one way of doing things that we were doing differently. After months of work, we started providing many of the same answers to the customers, but kept working to perfect standardization.

Not long after I completed the challenging assignment, a new position was posted as manager over both Help Desks. Since I worked so hard to standardize and oversee the two Help Desks over a year, and had developed a great relationship with the staff and employees, I applied for the position. I believed I was the best person for the job. A couple of months later, I was promoted into the position.

Next I was assigned to come up with a plan to resolve the telephone wait time problem. I suggested we stop the transfer of work until we get a handle on the workload. Gary agreed and put the work on hold.

We needed new technology if we were going to keep our customers happy. I started campaigning for a state-of-the-art phone system. I put together a proposal and submitted it to the Vice President.

A meeting was scheduled with the Help Desk and Telecommunications management to discuss my proposal. They suggested we purchase one system for the Minnesota office, with a tie-line for the California calls. Minnesota was the larger office and that's why the suggestion was made. We didn't like it but that was our best option. The proposal was then approved, and we implemented the system with the tie-line. Once the phone system was updated, I submitted a proposal to purchase a shared database. What a big improvement in the service to the customers. Eventually, we were able to get the California office a phone system.

I finally got to meet the VP. He said he wanted to put me in the Executive Leadership Program. I had no idea this was coming. I was excited. This would better my chance to advance in the company. I submitted the paperwork. Several months later, I was accepted into the program. God continued moving in my life.

All this was going on at the same time I was finishing up my classes for my master's degree in psychology and counseling, working on my dissertation on children with behavioral problems, working full time, working another 20 hours a week internship, completing my presentation for the Executive Leadership program, preparing to defend my dissertation, training to be a deacon, living on four hours of sleep, and working with my new manager Rod. Only by the Grace of God was I successful. However, after a couple of deacon meetings, the training was put on hold for about a year. God knew how much I could handle.

Two weeks before my dissertation was due, the professor assigned to review my paper said it did not flow and needed work. She asked if I had an editor. When I said no, she recommended one. I called her immediately. She took a week to edit my paper. Then I had to make the changes and send it back to the professor for approval. She took several days to get back to me. I was starting to panic. Finally, I got the call I had been waiting for. She had approved it and sent it to the board. It was two days before the deadline. God was looking out for me again. I called right away to set up the appointment to go before the board to defend my dissertation.

I took a week's vacation. I needed to clear my head. I came back ready to defend my paper in front of the board. I was so nervous. This would determine if I graduated. They asked lots of questions. God had prepared me and I was ready. Finally, it was over. The board asked if I would wait outside. I was on pins and needles waiting. The professor that I was assigned to came out. She looked at me, and said, "You passed." I was so excited; I gave her a big hug, and thanked her for all her help. Then we went back inside. We had additional discussion before I was finally dismissed.

My husband was waiting for me in the student lounge. I ran out and told him I had passed. He said, smiling, "I would have expected nothing different." I graduated a week later.

I had just graduated from graduate school, and my husband had just retired. We had planned a seven-day cruise to the Hawaiian Islands. We purchased our tickets through a travel agency, and purchased the insurance. I was finishing up my executive leadership program and had to be back in town by a certain date. I contacted the travel agent and left messages several times inquiring about the return date. Two weeks before the cruise, I found out the date of return was the same day I had to be in class. I contacted the travel agent again. This time they answered. I explained my dilemma. I said, "I needed my ticket returning the day before the date of the ticket she had purchased." I didn't think it would be a problem because we had insurance. However, I found out I could only use the insurance if I was unable to attend due to illness and needed documentation. I asked for my money back. She said I couldn't get a refund. In the past I would have blown my top.

"Oh, you have to do something. I called and left messages several times before you purchased the tickets, and no one returned my call."

She kept saying there was nothing she could do. After I insisted because her office never returned my call, she said she would refund the money for the tickets but it would have to wait until after the trip. I don't know why I had to wait, but I waited. About two months after the trip, I received a check from the agency. It bounced. This was in October. I had to wait until December before we finally got a good check.

I ended up purchasing two tickets. I paid for one and the job paid for the other. I had to be in Washington DC, by noon that Monday. I had already booked my ticket for the trip to Hawaii returning to Minnesota. Since I had to change planes in Chicago, I booked the other ticket from Chicago to Washington DC. That flight would get me to DC by 10:30am which would give me enough time to get to class by noon.

When the cruise was over, we headed to the airport. I checked in and showed the agent my two tickets. I said, "I want my bags tagged for DC because I was not going to complete my trip to Minnesota." She started keying information into the system. A little while later she said

"That will be $900.00."

I was sure I didn't hear that correctly. "What?"

She repeated the amount.

"Why do I have to pay $900.00 when I already purchased two tickets totaling over $1,000.00."

"Ma'am, it's because you are not completing your trip to Minnesota."

"You're charging me $900.00 to tag my suitcase on the fight to DC?"

She kept repeating it was because I was not completing my trip to Minnesota.

"I have two tickets and I am not paying another dime. I want to speak to a manager." She called her manager over and explained the situation.

"Yes, you have to pay the additional money."

Head moving and finger wagging, I said "I am not paying any additional monies. I have already purchased two tickets. I'm not leaving until you tag by my bag for D.C."

We stood there, my husband and I holding up the line. I had my elbow propped up on the counter with my hand on the side of my face staring at the attendant and her boss.

The two of them kept whispering, and I kept staring. A customer behind us was getting restless, and started grumbling. Finally, the attendant relented.

I just stood there. She acted as if she was doing me a favor. I guess she wanted me to be grateful. While I stood there waiting for her to finish the transaction, she grabbed me by the chin and turned my face to look at her.

"Do you understand what we are doing for you?" I could have gotten angry because she grabbed my chin, but instead, I said, "Yes." I wasn't going to say thank you, though.

We proceeded to go to the gate. I put my bags on the roller. They pulled my bags aside and took the fruit. I forgot I couldn't bring fruit back from Hawaii. Then I was pulled over to be searched. I felt the ticket agent did it purposely because I didn't say thank you but calmly let them search me and then proceeded to the gate.

When we got to the gate, we found out the flight was delayed two hours. I started to get a little anxious. If I missed my connecting flight in Chicago, I would be late for class. I'm sitting on the seat praying and trying not to panic or get angry and this lady sitting across from us started talking. She said, "My dad is a pilot. He said we will get a tail wind and make up the time." I knew that was the Spirit of God calming me down and keeping me from getting angry.

The plane finally came. We boarded quickly. Shortly, we were in the air. We flew all night, and sure enough made up some of the time. But it was close.

I got off the plane about 8:45am. My next flight was leaving about 9:05am. I looked at the board, found my flight, kissed my husband goodbye, and took off like I had wings. The plane was some distance away. I didn't stop running until I reached the gate. I was out of breath. They were still boarding. I just happened to look across the way and there was my husband's flight. However, he had time before his departure so he was taking his time. We didn't even know our flights were across from each other. When we kissed, I went in one direction, and he went in another. I got on my fight and soon we were back in the air. The flight left on-time, and we landed on-time. By the time I got to the baggage claim, my bag was coming around. I grabbed it quickly, silently thanked the Lord, and headed outside to hail a cab.

I arrived at the academy around 11:00am, showered, changed my clothes, and headed to class. I got to class about 11:45am with 15 minutes to spear. I kept praying and trusting God, because Murphy's Law was at hand. Had I let anger control me, things would have turned out differently. Instead, I kept praying and talking to the Lord, and passed that test.

Chapter 20
The Challenges

One day I was sitting in my office and Rod came in and said that since I was in the Executive Leadership program, he wanted me to take an assignment in the Production Operations area. I was excited about the assignment, but didn't realize he wanted me to start effective immediately. I said to him it would be too much for me right now. I was finishing up my final classes for my master's degree, working on my dissertation, finishing up my internship, and working on my final presentation for the Executive Leadership Program which we had to present to the VP's. I didn't tell him I was also in training to be a Deacon. He was not happy and gave me two days to decide. Two days later he came back for my decision. I said, "I weighed the pros and cons and decided that it was not the right time, but would be happy to take the assignment in three months."

Then he asked, "What if I mandate you?"

"If you mandate me them I have no choice."

"Then I mandate you take the assignment, and you will start effective Monday," Rod replied. I had two days and a weekend to get ready. I silently prayed to the good Lord for direction.

Before close of business, however, our Vice President interceded, and I did not have to be reassigned.

Rod's next attempt to sabotage me came soon enough. He came into my office one morning and said I had to move, that he was assigning me to the office inside the operations department. "No problem," I said. I wasn't going to let him ruffle me. He said he needed me to move right away.

The next day, I packed up and moved out.

About five months later, Rod sent the building manager to tell me he needed my space, and I would have to move again. A couple of days later, I was informed that I would be moving to the conference room in the hallway as soon as they get furniture.

My employees started warning me, saying the conference room that they planned to move me to was near the bathrooms, and often smells permeated the conference room. It was also not soundproof.

I decided to take a look for myself and couldn't believe what I found. This "office" didn't have any of the furniture other managers' offices had. It had a cubicle in the corner that didn't have room for my files or personal belongings. I could not believe what I was seeing.

I started to let them move me, and file a complaint. But after some fasting and praying, God gave me the answer.

By now, I had a new manager, Bob. However, Bob's office was domiciled in Raleigh. I sent an email to Rod and Bob. The email went something like this: "I will not be moving from the office I'm in until I get an office comparable to the one I have." Bob called as soon as he got the email. He said he was going to schedule a meeting with Rod to discuss the issue.

Bob called back to say he would be flying in Monday morning. When he arrived, I took him to the conference room to show him my new office. Rod was coming out as we were headed in. We were cordial, said hello, and headed into the office. Bob could not believe it when I showed that my previous office was still vacant.

We went to meet with Rod. God had prepared me for the fight, and I was ready. We walked in his office and sat down. He started small talk. At the same time, I was having self-talk about what I thought about him and his small talk. Then he said, "Oh, by the way, you don't have to move."

I asked him to repeat himself.

He said it again. "You don't have to move. We found another office we can use."

He took the wind right out of my sails. I was all prepared to blow him out of the water with all his foolishness. I kept trying to get my words out but God would not let me speak. I kept having self-talk with God saying, "I just want to say," but I couldn't get the words out. When you trust and believe in God, He will prepare you but you may not have to say a word. I believe the preparation is His way of seeing if we are going to be obedient.

A couple of months after our meeting, Rod walked into my office and said they were going to build me an office inside the Help Desk area. This was the suggestion I'd once presented to the building manager but he said it was not an option. However, when you are obedient to God and trust Him, He works everything out. When it was completed, it was better than the previous offices I occupied. It was my blessing from God. I prayed over it before I moved in. After I moved in, many people came to discuss matters and I would end up praying for them. I was never interrupted when I was praying. I knew God's angels were watching over me and my office. I couldn't stop thanking God for His blessing.

However, no sooner than I settled in, though, Bob started having issues with every decision I made. He would send emails asking questions, or wanting answers, and no matter what I said, I could not satisfy him. As long as I responded, he kept asking dumb questions. If I ignored him, he would email again saying please respond. If I called him to explain, he would say he understood, and then maybe a week later, I would get the same email asking for a response. He would also get on the weekly conference call and embarrass me in front my staff. Since he was the manager, I tried to be respectful.

I made copies of all of his emails and waited for an opportunity to discuss them. My opportunity finally came. Gary was retiring. I called Bob to ask if I could work out of the Raleigh office that week so I could attend the retirement party. To my surprise, he said yes. I flew into Raleigh the weekend before the party but didn't check into the hotel until Monday evening because technically, Monday was my travel day. Bob knew I was in town. He tried to call me on Monday, but I missed his call.

When I called him back, the first words out of his mouth were "Where have you been?"

I reminded him I was on my travel day and was just getting to the hotel. Then he said he was giving me a lower merit rating than I thought I deserved. I just said okay because I was on my time, and I was tired and hungry. Besides, I wanted to discuss the rating face to face. I had also brought the emails to discuss with him as well.

He was busy Tuesday morning, but I was determined to talk with him that day no matter how long I had to wait. After the luncheon, I marched into his office, and shut the door. First, I asked about the rating. He couldn't give me a straight answer. He said No, he was not changing the rating. I told him I was going over his head because I deserved better. I also discussed his attitude. He acted as if he didn't know what I was talking about and said that he would have to see the emails. To his surprise, I presented them.

He looked shocked and said he didn't realize he was doing it. I let him know I would no longer tolerate his disrespectful behavior. He said we needed to work on our communication, and I agreed. I left his office and went directly to his managers' office. I made an appointment with his secretary. The only appointment available was at the end of the day. I said, "That's fine."

When we met, he said he had received several complaints about my manager and would handle it. We talked about my rating. He said he would see what he could do to get it changed. I thanked him and left. I got the merit I thought I deserved. I thank God for giving me the courage to stand up for it.

My husband had traveled with me and was waiting at the hotel. We picked up dinner, and I said, "Let's go to happy hour." I had a tough day and just needed to unwind. It felt good to finally get that off my chest. My mom always said, "If something bothers you get it off your chest."

The next week, Bob came to my office and sat down. He apologized for the way he had been acting and reiterated that we needed to communicate better. I accepted his apology and agreed again that we needed to work on our communication.

At this time, my deacon's training restarted, and it was intense. There was a lot to learn before the ordination. My husband and I were in training together, which was nice. This was more than being ordained. It was about passing another test.

The ordination process included being tested by five male preachers. When I heard this, my unconscious mind alerted me. The pain in my chest was unbearable. I couldn't sleep. I talked with God. He helped me understand that I wasn't totally healed. Sitting in front of the preachers would complete my healing process. The more I thought about it, the more uneasy I became. I decided to share my story with my pastor.

I was still having pains, and continued to talk with God. I really needed to pass this test so I could move on with my life. I finally realized the pains were growing pains. I asked the Lord to help me deal with the pain.

As the training continued the thought of sitting in front of those preachers became easier. On ordination day, I answered the questions with confidence. Not that

I knew all the answers, but when I answered, I was confident. They dismissed us to discuss our responses. Then they called us back in and said we passed. That was a special moment. I was happy and excited. Not only had I passed the test for ordination, I passed my test of sitting in front of authority figures without freezing up or having anger towards them. I thank God for healing me and giving me the confidence to face my assailant.

Bob was put on special projects and Henry was assigned as my new manager. However, Henry was domiciled in California and started making decisions for the California office without consulting me. I managed both Help Desks so it was difficult to work with someone constantly undermining me and keeping me in the dark. He wanted to make decisions without consulting me, and that wasn't really a problem, but once he made a decision I should be brought into the loop. If Henry thought I would disagree with him, he wouldn't include me.

Of course, we had a "Come to Jesus" meeting. One afternoon I called him to talk. He started screaming at me like a crazy man and said I was disrespecting him. Then he slammed the phone down.

Ten minutes later the phone rang back.

"Deborah, this is Henry. Let's forget what just happened."

By the end of the conversation, he understood that he could not get away with bypassing me. After that call, he started including me in the Help Desk decisions, even if he didn't like what I had to say. Henry was short lived and then I had an interim manager.

Chapter 21

My Way Out

It was mid-year evaluation, and I had to meet with the interim manager to discuss my accomplishments.

As we discussed my performance, he asked "Would you be willing to take a reassignment to manage the Production Operations?" This was the same department Rod tried to mandate me to manage years before. To his surprise, I agreed to take the assignment. I was tired of working with a group of mangers that kept working against me.

God had given me an out and I was going to take it. This turned out to be the break I needed, just at the right time.

I transferred right away, and was assigned several outstanding projects. One was a major upgrade of the system and was already in progress when I began working within the department. The deadline was just months away, so I had to work quickly.

First I set up a meeting with the staff. I needed to find out why they weren't meeting target dates. One of the employees said it couldn't be accomplished because they had to rely on other departments. Another employee said they were setting me up to fail because there was no way the project could be completed by the deadline date.

I looked at him and said, "We don't fail. What do we need to do to meet our deadline?"

They looked at me with disbelief. I told them not to worry and to leave the other departments to me. We discussed what was needed. Thank God. I had a great staff.

I met with the manager of the other department. I asked if they would give our project priority so we could meet the deadline. She said she would meet with her staff and get back to me.

I didn't wait for her to get back to me. I sent her an email, and copied in the Headquarters managers and VP thanking her for meeting with me and agreeing to discuss giving our project priority. I put a plan together and submitted it to my new manager requesting overtime for my staff. He approved the overtime, and said I needed to send weekly progress reports. When I sent the weekly reports, I would include the other department, and the Headquarters managers and VP. I would also annotate if we were waiting on the other department to move forward.

This worked great. No one wanted to be singled out as the one holding up the project. Everyone started staying on task and we completed the project a month before it was due.

The staff felt good that they completed the project before the deadline, and said they couldn't have done it without me. I rewarded them by giving them a pizza party. I invited some of the people that helped, and brought donuts for the other department. My new manager, his boss, and the new VP were all very impressed. The VP came to one of our staff meeting, and commended me on doing a great job.

At the time I was transferred, I didn't know anything about Production Operations. I had been working for the interim manager and was desperate to get out of that situation – there was nothing but sabotage and derailment working for him. Here I had a great staff that worked with me to accomplish the goals. The employees were right, though – this position had been given to me to set me up for failure. But the interim manager didn't know me.

He couldn't believe we completed the project ahead of schedule. He was also shocked that I was able to get the other departments to work with us. I was glad he got to see who I really was and my work ethic.

His boss sent me a monetary award for completing the project ahead of schedule. Usually awards are presented at staff meetings, but the interim manager quietly eased into my office and handed it to me. He didn't want anyone to know.

I was on assignment for six months, and I was enjoying the staff and the work. It wasn't a surprise when I was offered the job. I really wasn't ready to retire, but my mom was aging and I needed to move closer to her. My husband and I were searching for a home in North Carolina.

I tried several times to get jobs in the Raleigh office but was unsuccessful. When I discussed it with the Headquarters' manager he said, "That's not a place you want to be." There were at least two occasions I was offered opportunities that mysteriously didn't work out. I heard from one of the managers that the VP would not approve the assignment.

I was eligible to retire, and after much prayer and talk with God, He assured me that I could retire. He had always taken care of me and would continue. I submitted my papers. When Headquarters called asking for my manager's name, they said they had to inform him I was retiring. I said I didn't want anyone to know. She said I had to give them two weeks' notice. I didn't need to do anything anymore. I was retiring. But two weeks before I retired, I told one of the managers I trusted. I said, "If you tell anyone I will call in sick and not come back." He said he had to tell the VP. I told him to go ahead but please let her know I didn't want anyone else to know.

A couple of days later I get an email from the VP that put me in the Executive Leadership program. He said he heard I was retiring, and wanted to thank me for the work I had done to make them successful. On my last day, the headquarters manager flew in just to say goodbye. I was surprised he took time out of his busy schedule to say goodbye and thank me for my role in the success of our department. I said the only thing I asked in return was to get my bonus pay. He said, "Don't worry I will make sure it happens." I thanked him and started packing to leave.

And then I retired. I just walked out of the door. When the interim manager knew anything, I was gone.

.

Chapter 22

The Turning Point

I never looked back. I got in my car and I just screamed to the top of my lungs. I couldn't stop thanking God. He had guided me though my work journey and now I was retired.

Joe said he wanted to live between Greensboro and Raleigh. He looked on the map and picked the city of Mebane. Several builders came up, but he soon narrowed his focus on this one builder. He requested information about their homes and was sent a package. He stayed in contact with the builder through email.

We kept saying we were going to make an appointment to see the models. We came down several times during those two years, but never made the appointment.

Soon after I retired, I had to give up my deacon's assignment. God had other plans. My husband and I became caretakers. Although, I loved my deacons' assignment and visiting the sick and shut-in (because many times they also lifted my spirits), helping to take care of my family became the priority. Although this wasn't the plans my husband and I had in mind for retirement, it was God's plan.

One day as I was leaving the nursing home, the elevator stopped and one of the patients got on. She was admiring my outfit, saying how beautiful I looked. I thanked her, and we talked until the elevator stopped on the ground floor. I was leaving the building and she was going outside for some fresh air. As we headed to the door, she stopped, turned to me and recited this scripture:

"For I know the plans I have for you, declares the Lord, plans to prosper you and not to harm you, plans to give you hope and a future." (Jeremiah 29:11)

Only God could have known how I was feeling that day. He sent one of His own with that message for me. She caught me off guard. I was doing my servant work, making sure the sick and shut-in got communion. But it turned out to be a blessing for me as well, as it often was. I had been praying for God to give me a sign. We wanted to sell our home and move, and things were not going the way we had planned. So her message gave me the strength and courage to "Wait once again on the Lord."

Just before we put the house on the market, my husband contacted the builder again and said we would be visiting soon. However, the house sold so quickly, we didn't have time to make the trip until just before the closing.

We fell in love with the first house, but I wanted four bedrooms. The builder took us to see another model. It was my dream home. Everything I had prayed for and more. I forgot all about the first house. It was nice, but the second one was even nicer, and my dream home. If I didn't have faith in God, I would have settled for the first one because I would have said we couldn't afford the second one. I wanted it and I told God I wanted it, and God made it possible. We missed the ground breaking because we were in Minnesota. However, once we returned, we came by every week sometimes twice a week to visit our home. We watched it being built from the ground up. I was not interested in building at first because we had sold our home, and was homeless in a nice way. We were again blessed by God because my husband's aunt was out of town for eight months and invited us to stay at her home. It was nice and we were very comfortable there.

When you are so use to having your own place, you just long for it, and I didn't want to wait 4-5 months to build a home. But as I watched the progression, I got excited. I was glad I went along with my husband's plan to build.

It was like a miracle watching the pieces come together.

We were traveling a lot those days, but it was returning home from Joe's aunt's funeral when my anger was sorely tested. We'd boarded the flight in New York and had to change flights in Chicago going to Minnesota. The flight was scheduled to leave at 4:05pm and we would get home in plenty of time to wash clothes and prepare for our flight to California early the next morning. The flight to Chicago arrived late, but we still had a few minutes before boarding. I had to use the bathroom so I told my husband to go ahead just in case the flight was boarding. I came out of the bathroom and rushed down to the boarding gate. I arrived at the gate about 3:45pm.

Things didn't feel right. I asked my husband if they were boarding. He said he had not heard anything or seen anyone boarding. I walked up to the counter and asked the attendant. She said, "The doors were already closed." I asked, "How could they be close? The flight is not scheduled to leave until 4:05pm." I told the attendant I needed to be on that plane. No matter what I said they would not open the door. The attendant said we had to go to customer service to be booked on the next flight. We went to customer service. The attendant said the next flight was six hours later. I could have lost it but I think for a former angry person, I handled myself pretty well. I did have a few choice words for a few of the rude attendants. However, there was one attendant that went out of her way to help us. That was only God because He knew if I had to deal with the rude attendant much longer I probably would have lost it.

Six hours later, our plane came. The attendant announced on the PA system to tear our tickets before we line up to make things move faster. We tore our tickets and waited on line to board. One of the passengers didn't tear her ticket and the attendant got an attitude. He asked in a nasty tone, "Would you tear your ticket?"

I didn't like the way he talked to the passenger. When I stepped up to the attendant I gave him my torn ticket.

"You made us wait six hours now you want us to do your job too?"

"Ms., if you want to go to Minnesota tonight, you better keep walking."

My husband turned around and said, "And who is going to stop her?" After six hours of waiting we were frustrated and in no mood for nonsense.

"You'd better keep walking,"

Joe replied, "And what are you going to do if I don't?"

I turned to Joe and told him to just keep going, this man was not worth it. We got on the plane and the flight attendant asked in a pleasant voice, "How was your day?"

"Not good. This airline has gotten on my last nerve," I replied.

We took our seats. Just before takeoff, I saw the attendant that took our tickets talking to the flight attendant on the plane. He walked to the back where we were seated.

"I bet he's coming to say something to us," I whispered to Joe.

"No I don't think so."

He walked past us and went to the back of the plane. But on his way back, he stopped at our seats.

"Mrs. Warren."

I looked up. "Yes?"

"The next time you threaten me you will be thrown off the plane."

I looked him in the eyes. "I didn't threaten you. I said you made us wait six hours and now you want us to do your job too."

He clearly didn't like my response. He asked us to get off the plane.

"We are not moving," Joe responded.

"I'll be back."

I turned my head to the window. I started praying. I said, "Lord, please forgive me for opening my big mouth. I was wrong, Lord, you know I need to get home because I have an early flight in the morning." Then I sat and waited for the outcome.

I saw him up front talking with the flight attendant, then the pilot came out of the cock-pit and they were all talking. Then he got off the plane. A little while later, his manager comes on the plane. He came up to us and asked what happened. We told him the story and he said that was no reason to throw us off the plane. Said I was right it was not our job to tear the tickets. He apologized and said there would be two tickets waiting for us when we arrived in Minnesota. We thanked him and he got off the plane.

Then the flight attendant came over to our seats.

"Mr. and Mrs. Warren, come with me. We are moving you to first class. Do you have bags? I will take them."

We followed him. No sooner than we sat down, the pilot comes out of the cockpit kneels down in front of us and apologized for the rude behavior of the attendant. He gave us his business card and told us if necessary, he would vouch for the attendant's rude behavior. God is so good! All I could do was sit there and thank Him because I could see Him at work. God had blessed us with First Class Service. *Thank you, Lord.*

We finally arrived in Minnesota around midnight. We stopped by the counter but there were no tickets, only a write up of our behavior.

When I got home, I wrote a letter to the airlines and to the FAA as well, because I was sure they were not aware the airline was leaving prior to departure time. We receive an apology and two round-trip tickets. I told my husband that I would never fly that airline again. My husband used his ticket a couple of months later, but I never used mine. I refused to deal with an airline whose customer service is so rude. I managed customer service for many years, and I would never allow the employees to get away with rudeness.

Chapter 23

Waiting on the Lord

When I retired in 2010, my husband and I were making plans to sell our home and move to North Carolina. I say 'making plans,' but we were trying to move ahead of God's plan, and guess what? Our plans were delayed. God had to get our attention and remind us that we had left Him out of the plan, and therefore our plan would be delayed. I realized I was trying to work my plan without God. I just wanted to sell our home and get out of Minnesota. I asked God to forgive me for trying to move ahead of His plan and give me the patience to "wait on Him." I prayed but nothing happened. I prayed harder and ask God to give me the strength to wait on Him. I wanted His will and not mine. During our wait, we met my sister, Mary.

A prayer God had answered. She and my mom attended the same Church. One day I was at Church with mom and she introduced us. She resembles my sister Shirley. Whenever we ran into each other at Church she was always cordial. I felt a connection.

To slow us down and remind us He is in charge, God gave us care-giving assignments for all of 2011. I was not happy about the delay but accepted it because I know God knows best.

In 2012, God blessed our plans. We put the house on the market, and three days later we had a buyer. We had to move fast. We laid out our plan and focused on the things that needed to be accomplished right away. Our plans were working this time because God was in them. The immediate plans were to find a mover, storage for our household goods, and get a post office box for the mail. We traveled to North Carolina. We got there on a Sunday night. The next morning, we went out to find storage, and get a post office box. To my surprise, we got the post office box right away. Surprised because I was told it would take up to two weeks because we didn't live in State. An hour later, we had a place to store our belonging. Every time we accomplished a goal, I thanked God. Things were happening so quickly. I knew it was because God was in the plan. This is how God works when you don't try to get ahead of Him. He was guiding us every step of the way.

The house had to pass appraisals and inspections. The first was the truth and lending inspection to get the house on the market. The inspection was done on a Monday, passed and the house went on the market that

Wednesday. The second inspection was the buyer's inspection. We had some electrical work to update before the buyer would continue with the purchase. We called an electrician and the work was completed in three days. After we completed the updates, the bank had to do an appraisal/inspection to see if the house was worth the asking price because the buyer had a FHA loan. All this was completed before we went on our trip to North Carolina. We were gone a week. When we returned, we got the news the house had passed FHA appraisal/inspection. We set the closing date. This was all completed in less than two months. So you see how fast we had to move. We had an excellent mover, and our household goods were delivered on-time, and unbroken. Only God could perform like that. I thank Him all the time because He keeps on blessing us.

After getting over being upset because we were delayed, I was able to see that we were delayed because God had heard my prayers. He was just looking out for our best interest. The housing market was really bad. People kept saying the house probably wouldn't sell because of it. I would just say under my breath "the devil is lair." But as I continued to pray and study God's word I realized he can see over the mountains and he prepares us for what we can't see. The market still wasn't that great when we finally put the house on the market. However, it was the right time because it was just starting to turn around. I was hearing it was "a buyers' market, not a sellers' market."

But the devil is a liar. I continued to trust God. As I grew spiritually, I trusted God more and more. I learned to wait on Him if things didn't go my way. It's so good to be able to give it all to God and trust Him to take care of you.

Not only did He sell our home in three days, He gave us a place to stay. My husband's aunt invited us to house sit while she was out of town. "Only God's timing." We sold our house so quickly; we didn't have time to look for a place of our own. God knew we didn't want to rush into anything, and prepared a comfortable place for us while we looked for a new home. It wasn't our home but it felt so much like home. God is so good to His children.

Had we tried in 2010, we probably would have had to take the house off the market two or three times. That would have really been frustrating. God knows the right timing for everything.

While we waited, God blessed us with another surprise. We were in Myrtle Beach for our Family Reunion. It was July 4, 2012 weekend. Mary called my mom. She had heard we were in town. She said my father's out-of-wedlock son was in town and wanted to meet us. Mom told her we would be at the park. She brought him there.

When I saw him, I got weak in the knees. He was the spitting image of our dad. I thought I was seeing a ghost.

Dad died in 2003, two weeks before his 90th birthday. I was still living in Minnesota when he died. It was a Sunday evening when I got the call. It was my mom. She said she had just found out he was dead, and the funeral was Tuesday. She asked, "Are you coming? Your sister said she is coming." I said it was too short a notice so I would not be attending. I asked her to get me an obituary. I wasn't upset that I couldn't attend; we didn't have a bond. I wanted the obituary because it would provide family history information. Of course, none of the outside children were listed.

Whenever I'd asked my father for information about his family, he seemed uncomfortable. One day he said, "Everything is in John's name." I made it clear I was only seeking information for medical reasons, and I didn't need or want anything from him. He said he didn't mean it the way it sounded. He just wanted me to know. Again, "I said, I don't need anything from you."

My brother was so handsome. We bonded on the spot. We exchange numbers and promised to keep in touch. It felt so good to have a big brother. During our conversation, we discovered my sister Shirley and brother are the same age, and the sister Mary that goes to mom's church and I are the same age. We just shook our heads in disbelief, and starting singing "Papa Was a Rollin' Stone." He was dating both women at the same time, and he was married.

When I hired my mom's home attendant, I found out that she knew my dad. His daughter-in-law is her god-mother, and she knew his sons and their children. One day she took my husband and I to visit my father's grave. I had mentioned that I wasn't able to attend the funeral. After we left the gravesite, she took us to meet some of my father's people. We stopped at his niece's house. She said she had met my sister and I before. My nephews lived across the road in my dad's house. She called them over to meet us. They hesitated at first because they said the way she was calling them they thought they had done something wrong.

"This is your Aunt Deborah."

"Oh, wow. Grandpa told us we had an aunt that lived in Minnesota."

"That would be me." I smiled.

My nephews stood there staring at me. Then one said, "You look just like Cathy."

"Who is Cathy?"

"That's Grandpa's other daughter."

"Where does she live? I want to meet her."

"She lives in Georgetown."

My dad had said there were two sisters but he was the father of only one of the girls and since I had already met Mary, who looks so much like my sister, I assumed she was the one. But now I'm puzzled.

It was two years later before we met. I was taking my niece to the grocery store, and ran into my sister Mary. She said Cathy was in town for the weekend. "She is at the Church right now if you want to stop by."

I dropped my niece off and drove to the Church.

Mary looked up when I walked in and smiled as she pointed.

"That's your sister Cathy."

We embraced, and talked for a few minutes. Their younger sister had come to pick her up, and she had to leave. She said we would get together before she left so she could fill me in. *Hmm. Fill me in?*

I was anxious and wanted to know what she had to say. They introduced me to the younger sister Joy. She said she knew me. I asked how she knew me and she said she had attended my mom's 80th birthday party with her mom. I was stunned. I didn't know they knew each other.

Now I *really* wanted to meet with them to find out the details. We planned to meet Sunday. They said they would cook dinner at the younger sister's house and we would all meet there. Wow, this was exciting.

Mary agreed to pick me up. Since I hadn't heard from her, I called when I thought she was home from Church but got no answer. I called several more times, still no answer. I wondered what happened. By late afternoon, I gave up and went to the community baseball game.

Early the next morning, Mary called to say we were going to meet at Red Lobster at three o'clock. She said she had worked all weekend with the NAACP program at her Church, and went home and passed out.

We all met at the Red Lobster, and by the time they finished telling me the story of our lives, I couldn't eat. Cathy is the same age as my sister Shirley and brother Bill I met four years ago. This meant that my father had at least three women pregnant at the same time, and that he was with at least four women, because he was also married.

When I heard this, I told them we should go dig him up and stomp his bones to pieces. We laughed but it was mind-blowing to listen to the story. They also said my mom and their mom were good friends. So that's why she was at my mother's 80th birthday party. I was saddened to think my mom could fall into a trap like that. She just didn't seem like the type to me. My sisters also told me their mother had 7 children, and had given all of them away except one of the sons. I then told them my mother had planned to give me away too but when I was born she said she couldn't do it. When I met my brother Bill, he said that he was given away, too. That must have been the thing to do in those days instead of abort the baby. Maybe it was best for them at the time, but no one thought of the effects it would have on the children. My sisters said their mother was a humdinger and the world owes her nothing. Mary said that the mother told her two different men were her father, my dad being one and said she told her children her father was dead. Wow, we were thinking Mary was our sister, and Cathy was the one my dad said was not his. This is mind blowing because Mary looks like my sister, and I look like Cathy. It also makes me wonder what my mom was like back in the day. But I will never know. The kicker is that the two sets of children are four years apart which mean they both were dating this married man for a long time even though they knew he was married. It's no wonder families keep the past hushed up. Lord, would I love to have a conversation with them to understand what was their maladjustment? I thank God for finally allowing us to meet. Ever since my father told me about them I wondered if I would ever meet them and God made it possible.

We decided since we all were going to be in town July 4, 2016 weekend to have a family reunion cookout. We didn't believe our oldest brother John would show up but Cathy thought maybe she could convince him.

A month later, I was back in Myrtle Beach and excited about our reunion cookout. It was held at my sister Mary's house. Too excited to sleep, I was up early. I was going to spend time and bond with my sisters and brother. I couldn't wait until three o'clock. I showered, and had a cup of tea. I was too excited to eat. The phone rang. It was Mary. She wanted to know if we could come earlier because my brother wanted to move the time to one o'clock.

My sister and I were glad because my mother's family was having a cookout too and we wanted to attend. We arrived at one o'clock. We were the first to arrive. Then Cathy arrived. I introduced her to my sister. We talked for a while. Then I called my brother to see where he was. The phone went to voice mail. We assumed he was on the way.

My brother finally shows up about forty-five minutes later. He said he changed the time so we would be there by 3pm, and that his wife is always late and just assumed we would be too. My nephews from one of my father's children with his wife also came. My 81-year-old brother John didn't come. We had so much fun laughing and talking and getting to know one another. By the time we finally decided to leave, it was 7:30pm. We had talked so much, and enjoyed each other's company and bond we lost track of time. My brother invited us to a party he was having the next day for his wife's birthday. I said, "I'll be there." My sister said she would too. When we finally got back to my mother's family one of my cousins said, "Ya'll go back were you come from, coming here this late." We all laughed and explained that we see them all the time, but we were bonding with long lost family. My cousin waved her hand and walked away, but she understood.

The next day we spent the day with them again. They had rented a villa for the week. The menu was seafood. The company and food was good. We met more cousins. By the time, we got back it was 9:30pm. Before we left, we stopped by my dad's niece's house. She was so excited to see us all together. It was a joyous two days. I am looking forward to hanging with them again and again. I never thought I would meet that side of the family, but we don't know God's plan. I'm so glad He allowed us to meet.

Chapter 24

Life is a Bunch of Projects

After years and years of life's ups and downs, trials and tribulations, good times and bad, I have come to the conclusion that life is a bunch of projects. Now when God gives me an assignment, I look at it as a project. A project has a start and finish date, and you have to make plans to accomplish it. It's the same as an assignment from God, you have a start and finish date, and you have to make plans to accomplish it. However, with God's assignments, you never know the start or finish date until God is ready for you to know. When you get the assignment, you have to start making plans. Your plans may not be God's plans and you might have to make adjustments. If you don't make the necessary adjustments to stay on course with God's plan, you will be starting over. You will continue to start over until you are on track with God's plan.

We've been in our new home for four years now, and I am so happy. I love my screened-in porch. The porch is where I spend my time with God when the weather is nice. I keep myself busy as my mom's power of attorney, writing my story, and selling Mary Kay. I was ready to retire, but wanted to do something different, but didn't want it to feel like work. When the opportunity came along to sell Mary Kay I jumped on it. It has provided me so much growth.

I always wanted to be a public speaker and Mary Kay is preparing me for that. I'm going to just keep praying and watching to see what God has next for me. My husband has been doing ancestry research since he retired. During his search, we found out that my family originated from North Carolina. When we moved here, it felt like home. As I ride down US highway 70, it reminds me so much of the route we took when we traveled by bus from New York to Myrtle Beach each summer. The small towns, the gas station stores where the bus stopped to let the people on and off, and the old-style houses. My family originated from Shallotte, NC.

The first summer I joined Mary Kay we went on a retreat to Ocean Isle Beach. As we were driving up to the beach, I saw a sign saying Shallotte, NC six miles. I yelled out, "I'm home!" I didn't know why I wanted to move to North Carolina. I just did. But as we continued our research, it all came clear. God was taking me back to familiar grounds. My ancestors from Shallotte are all dead now, but I feel their presence all around me.

When I was young, I remember sending my grandma some sunflower seeds that I had order. She planted them and when I visited her that summer, she took me to the place she had planted them. I was excited to see how big and tall they had grown. They looked like a bunch of faces shinning down on me. I smiled, and they seemed to smile back. When people would stop by and admire the sunflowers, my grandma would say Deb sent them to me. From that day on I loved sunflowers, and every time I see them I think about grandma. Last year the pastor gave everyone a pack of sunflower seeds and told us to go home and plant them and watch them grow. I was so excited. I gave them to Joe and asked him to plant them. He said it wasn't the right time of year.

"But the pastor told us to plant them now." He waited. He finally planted them but they never bloomed. I was disappointed because I wanted them to bloom so I could be reminded of grandma. He went to the store and bought sunflower seeds. Boy, everyday they grew taller and taller. I went out every day to talk to them.

Then one day I went out and a flower had bloomed. It looked just like the ones in my grandma's garden. It was smiling down on me and I smiled back. "Hello Grandma."

God sent me the flowers to remind me of grandma and how good she was to me. They are always smiling and I will cherish them until the sun withers them away. Two summers now I have enjoyed my sunflowers, and can't wait to see them smiling at me next summer.

Epilogue

I attended a documentary studies workshop on how to write a memoir. At the end of the workshop, the instructor asked the students "What have you learned from your writings?" She stated that sometimes in the middle of your writing you might have an epiphany, meaning something becomes clear to you. As one of the women shared her story, my epiphany became so clear. I realized I had been grieving for a very long time. Fifty-five years ago, when my mom took me away from my grandparent's home and move us to New York, I was devastated, and in the blink of an eye I had lost the only parents I knew. Grief-stricken, I hurt, and the anger boiled inside. Then we joined St. James Baptist Church the preacher reminded me of my grandfather. I found myself looking for his attention because he was always looking at me and would often smile. I thought I had found a fill-in for my grandfather. I was always looking to him to see if he was looking at me. I just needed to see that smile. When I discovered him looking at me, he would smile and I would smile back. He was giving me some needed attention, and I was happy. Sometimes he would give me a hug or put his hand around my shoulder and talk to me. It felt loving and made me happy until that night.

When I heard God say run, I ran. I grieved the loss of my grandfather fill-in. Grief and anger continued to overwhelm me because my mom and deacon decided to do nothing.

I grieved when I found out my mom didn't want me even though she couldn't give me away after I was born. I grieved because I was a middle child and could rarely get the attention I needed. I grieved because I felt unwanted. Then I got pregnant and lost mom's attention and the grief became unbearable. I grieved the death of the love hate relationship with my daughter's father. Grief was my world. But through my pain and grief, God was always with me. He gave me hope. Even though I knew the struggle would continue. I had hope. The sparkle in my life was being lit by hope.

The grief, anger, hurt, and pain lingered but I kept fighting through it. Doors kept opening and I kept working through my grief pain and anger. I couldn't stop fighting for my life. I landed a great job while still fighting through my grief and pain.

I worked hard, got several promotions, while earning a two-year degree, a bachelor's and master's degree all in psychology. I majored in psychology because I wanted to understand my grief, pain, and anger. During this time is when I took the "Boot Camp Training," and became aware that I had not dealt with the problem caused by the molestation. Once my eyes where opened I began to heal. I was trapped in anger and pain due to all my grief. I was only listening to the negative voice in my head and became trapped in fear. But now I'm free and will stay free until I die. I thank God for not giving up on me. I thank Him for opening my eyes and helping me see. I thank God for teaching me to listen to the positive voice. I thank God for freeing me from Satan's spell of negativity. I thank God for helping me understand it's all about His plans for my life. I thank God for the courage to write this book and using it as a ministry for others to understand that the struggle is real and will continue but with God nothing is impossible.

I'm still grieving because now my mom has dementia and I've lost her again. I've come to realize that grief is a major part of the process of life. Yes, it brings sadness and hurt but we all have to go through it. The Bible says there is "A time to be born and a time to die," Ecclesiastes 3:2. By this verse we know there will be grief. We all have to take the time to grieve but then get up and continue the struggle. The struggle leads to Hope (Hold On Pain Ends) and Hope leads to success, blessings, and freedom. So never give up on the struggle and never give up on God.

In 2003, I put it in my goals to write a book to tell my story. Here it is 2017 and I'm just finishing my manuscript. I got sidetracked many times, but God kept putting me back on track. It's God's plan, and He will make things possible if you believe.

May God bless all who read this book, and may it turn many lives around.

Deborah Warren

Deborah Warren uses her voice to serve God in Ministry to help others understand that it takes a relationship with God to build and sustain a successful future. It is her hope that this book will stretch her Ministry far beyond her hopes and dreams. Deborah loves God and does her best to spread that love to others. God has blessed Deborah and she just want to use her voice to give back. Deborah believes that God wants us all to use whatever gifts he gave us to help others. She also believes that if we all used our gifts to help others, the world would be a better place to live.

www.ingramcontent.com/pod-product-compliance
Lightning Source LLC
LaVergne TN
LVHW051257080426
835509LV00020B/3026